Nationalism and British Raj

S.R. Bakshi

ATLANTIC
PUBLISHERS & DISTRIBUTORS (P) LTD

ATLANTIC
PUBLISHERS & DISTRIBUTORS (P) LTD
7/22, Ansari Road, Darya Ganj, New Delhi
Tel.: +91-11-4077 5252, 2327 3880
E-mail: orders@atlanticbooks.com
Web: www.atlanticbooks.com

Published by Atlantic Publishers & Distributors (P) Ltd 2024

Disclaimer

- The author and the publisher have taken every effort to the maximum of their skill, expertise and knowledge to provide correct material in the book. Even then if some mistakes persist in the content of the book, the publisher does not take responsibility for the same. The publisher shall have no liability to any person or entity with respect to any loss or damage caused, or alleged to have been caused directly or indirectly, by the information contained in this book.
- The author has fully tried to follow the copyright law. However, if any work is found to be similar, it is unintentional and the same should not be used as defamatory or to file legal suit against the author.
- If the readers find any mistakes, we shall be grateful to them for pointing out those to us so that these can be corrected in the next edition.
- All disputes are subject to the jurisdiction of Delhi courts only.

Printed & bound in India by Atlantic Print Services

Preface

During the first global war the Punjab had become a centre of discontent on account of numerous economic and social reasons. The acute unemployment among the educated and uneducated youths of the region, the land revenue policy of the government leading to the awakening in the peasantry, the incident of Komagata Maru, the new awakening among Hindus and Sikhs of the Doab, the birth of revolutionary cult and a few other factors posed serious problems for the Raj. The Raj, on its part, passed repressive regulations leaving no chance for a common man to defend his basic rights. This led to an explosive situation by the end of the war.

The theme deals with the condition of the Punjab during the first global war, promulgation of repressive ordinances and regulations, the policy of the Raj, the ghastly tragedy at the premier town of the province, the reaction of bureaucracy, public opinion against the Raj and the new awakening in the hearts of the people leading to a final decision of the attainment of Swaraj. In the end an assessment of the events and a bibliography have been given.

I have consulted material from the National Archives of India, Sapru House Library and the Nehru Memorial Museum and Library, Delhi. I feel grateful to the authorities of these institutions for their help and co-operation during my research.

S.R. BAKSHI

Contents

Chapter 1

Global War and Punjab

The land of the Punjab stretching from Delhi to the borders of the North-West Frontier Province, with its alluvial soil irrigated by its prominent rivers and a network of canal system, had been the centre of numerous social, cultural, religious and political organizations. By a consistent flow of violent onslaughts on its land by the ambitious foreign rulers, a spirit of fearlessness, determination and sacrifice had been generated amongst the brave people of this province. With the establishment of the British rule in the Punjab in a couple of years after the demise of Maharaja Ranjit Singh, the anti-*Raj* feeling did not die down, rather it was utilised, at one time or the other, to make their nation free from the foreign yoke. The kind of model presented by the Kuka Movement; participation of prominent leaders in the freedom struggle under the banner of the Indian National Congress; the agitation and resentment in the canal-irrigated zone of the province and last but not the least, the patriotic role played by the *Ghadr* party[1] had a most significant impact on the thinking of the people who had begun questioning the role of *Raj* in terms of the benefits enjoyed by the people of India in services or otherwise.

The patriotic activities of the *Ghadr* party had inculcated much awakening amongst the people of the Punjab. Initially the initiative in this regard was taken by Lala Har Dayal and Bhai Parmanand who were responsible for imparting political education to Indians living in Vancouver and San Francisco. A committee was formed to collect money and run the paper *Ghadr* in Urdu and Punjabi. It soon became the spokesman of a sizable section of Indian society. In one of its issues, it stated, 'To-day there begins in foreign lands, but in our country's language, war against the English *Raj*. What is our name? Mutiny! *Ghadr* means mutiny. What is our work? Mutiny! Where will mutiny break out? In India ... The time is coming soon when rifles and blood will take the place of pen and ink. Brave men and worthy sons of India! Be ready with bullets and shots. Soon the fate of the tyrant will be decided and days of happiness and glory will dawn in India.'

It is thus evident that the *Ghadr* party had a revolutionary programme which had the following main objects in view, viz., to seduce Indian troops; to murder loyal subjects and officials; to loot Government treasury; to propagate through distribution of seditious literature; to commit dacoities; to procure arms and ammunition; to manufacture bombs, hand-grenades and other weapons; to establish secret societies which were to carry on anti-*Raj* propaganda; to loot police stations; to destroy railways, telegraph offices and other government establishments and, last but not the least, to mobilise the people living in the villages.

The fate of *Komagata Maru* and the oppression and repression its passengers had to bear were most tragic. On landing on the seashores of India, some of them were shot dead and a few of them were arrested and convicted. Those who could escape the fury of this repression made themselves busy in carrying on their revolutionary activities between 1914-15. A comprehensive effort was made to provoke mutiny among the Indian troops. Seditious pamphlets were systematically circulated and their emissaries secretly paid visits to some of the important cantonments in upper India. In Meerut, their activities were widely spread; bombs were taken to the cantonment area in order to kill European officers. In other areas, thirty-three violent activities including five murders were committed by members of the organization.[3]

The repressive measures of the government surpassed all limits. Their haunts and rendezvous were raided by numerous police parties, thoroughly searched and the party members were arrested. The punishments awarded to them were very severe, from deportation to hanging. On account of these stringent measures of the government combined with numerous other causes, the movement could not make much headway. But it left a significant impact on the people of the Punjab regarding the efficacy of the Raj and a feeling tinged with anti-Raj sentiments was imbibed amongst the uneducated peasantry which could be mobilized at a time when the province as a whole was to fight for a common cause at a later stage.

In the year 1914, the time of the commencement of the global war, the involvement of India as a subject-nation was unavoidable.[4] It became an essential function of each and every district, divisional and provincial official to see that there was the maximum response from his region towards the war-efforts of the British government. Such a necessity was that of the mobilisation of economic resources and manpower. To implement this kind of scheme war-loans were raised in one shape or the other and the public in India was sounded for investments in the government funds. The response was visible amongst the sections of people who were economically well-off. Besides, the dire need to have physically fit, although less educated, even uneducated, young men arose and the *Raj* had its hopeful expectations from the youths of the Punjab to safeguard British interests at various war-fronts. Michael O'Dwyer,[5] the Lieutenant-Governor of Punjab who was fully conversant with the courage, loyalty and physical prowess of a Punjabi soldier, called the Punjab, in a flattering tone, as the 'shield' and the 'sword band of India'.[6] He vigorously launched campaign at various levels to enlist recruits from various communities and in this task the response from the province was proverbial as it is clear from the Table given below:[7]

Name of Province	*Number of Recruits*
North-West Frontier	32,000
Punjab	3,50,004
United Provinces	1,42,000
Bombay	35,000
Bengal	6,000
Bihar and Orissa	8,000
Madras	46,000

Name of Province	Number of Recruits
Central Provinces	5,000
Assam	1,000
Burma	13,000
Ajmer	8,000
Native States under Government of India	80,000

The Punjab Recruitment Board consisting of Popham Young as chairman and prominent non-officials like Umar Hayat Khan, Raghbir Singh, Gujjan Singh, Mehdi Shah and Lal Chand as members recommended conscription throughout India. These recommendations were strongly supported by Michael O'Dwyer, although the central board administered by the government of India found it difficult to apply compulsion to the vast heterogeneous population of the country.[8]

This rejection of the board indeed was in no way an hindrance for the Punjab government to implement its scheme of conscription in a vigorous way. The scheme of recruitment was devised through various means. Recruiting *durbars* were held in the districts under the chairmanship of local British officials and prominent public men greatly assisted them in getting young men from schools, colleges and peasantry. Liberal rewards were granted to those who helped in this kind of recruitment.[9] According to Michael O'Dwyer, the Punjab was almost exhausted when the war came to an end. This was evident in August-September 1918 when a record number of young men over twenty-one thousand were enlisted in the army.[10] It has been estimated that 12,18,000 Indians and Gorkhas (including 7,91,000 combatants) were enlisted, and 14,57,000 (including 9,85,000 combatants) mobilized, during the First World War. The Punjab supplied about one-third of the Indian recruits and more than one-third of the total number who served. Of the combatants, both enlisted and mobilized, the Punjab supplied more than 40 per cent.[11]

The recruiting returns of the Multan district at the end of December 1917 stood at 759 or 1 in 586 of the male population. By the end of November 1918, the number rose to 4,636 or 1 in 93. Such a phenomenal record was possible only under severe methods of compulsion. The Commissioner of Multan Division stated, 'I am afraid with a few exceptions, the leading men in the district have not done their duty. Instead of enlisting members of their own families, they tried to buy or coerce men of lower stratum; objectionable methods of coercion were resorted to by some headmen with the result that in some cases public tranquility was disturbed.' The Commissioner of Ambala Division reported that, 'In order to make up the quota, the people resorted to the expedient of subscribing large sums to be given to young men to enlist, 500 or 1000 Rupees being the price of a recruit.'

'*Lambardars* had to furnish recruits on the penalty of forfeiting the *Lambardari* rights. Several were actually dismissed. Thus the value of a recruit goes to ₹ 500. Police sent up people to be bound down for keeping peace. Magistrates refused bail and sent them to the lock up, till they agreed to furnish recruits. Criminal prosecution was withdrawn on the accused agreeing to offer himself as a recruit.'

During the war, a number of Indian banks went bankrupt and this bankruptcy dealt a serious blow to numerous enterprises of the commercial houses, by affecting their capacity of production. 'This phenomenon was essentially a result of the colonial character of the economic structure in India, and of the lack of support for Indian banking capital from the state and the powerful British banks established in that country ... An enormous amount of food, agricultural and industrial raw materials, a large part of the output of the mining and metallurgical industries were exported, thus making it difficult to expand internal production. The British treasury attempted to cut down on its colossal war-time expenses by increasing the demands it made upon the ordinary Indian taxpayer. Not only the masses, but also the propertied classes in India suffered as a result of this policy. The financial and currency machinations of the colonial authorities and British businessmen gave rise to inflation (in 1914-1918 the overall total of currency notes in circulation nearly tripled) and to sharp rises in silver prices. Disruption of India's foreign trade links led to a sharp drop in the country's exports and imports. All this had a negative effect upon the country's economic position.'[12]

'Besides the prices of staple foods and produce were affected by all sorts of considerations, mostly inevitable. The autumn crop of 1914 was good, but the declaration of war suffered to send prices up, especially in the case of sugar. Cotton, however, suffered a severe slump, and was a 'drug,'[13] in the market that winter. . .' This kind of economic phenomenon had immediately affected the middle classes and people with limited means. People with fixed moderate incomes were most hard-hit in this direction and among them were the subordinate railway officials who were, therefore, discontented.'

When Lord Chelmsford took over as Viceroy of India in April 1916, the home government gave a serious thought over the recasting of the whole machinery which might prove more helpful in the management of war which was already about two years old.[14] It was felt that if the Indian Empire as a whole was to contribute a substantial share in the war, the organisation generally, and in particular that part of it engaged in raising manpower, must be recast in order to utilise the whole machinery and influence of the civil machinery as was then being done in Great Britain. In the autumn of the same year, when General Charles Munro who succeeded Beauchamp Duff as Commander-in-Chief pressed the same kind of opinion it was readily accepted by the Government of India.[15] This decision was welcomed by the Punjab Government. At the Viceroy's instance, the Lieutenant-Governor prepared a memorandum which showed how the military and civil machinery could be coordinated, giving instances of the evil results which had followed from the lack of such co-operation and of the failure of the military authorities to adapt their system, suitable enough for peacetime, to the new conditions created by the war.

'From February 1917, in the Punjab, and from June 1919 in the other provinces, the civil administration was directly associated with the military in the task of providing men and munitions; the recruiting organisation was rapidly expanded by the appointment of experienced civilians, official and non-official, with a knowledge of the people, as assistant to the military recruiting officers; Indian officials or non-officials of influence were employed on recruiting work in nearly every district; the territorial system of recruitment by which suitable men of every class could be enrolled in nearly every district was substituted for the old class system under which there were only four recruiting centres, Rawalpindi for Mohammedans; Amritsar for Sikhs, Jullundur for Dogras, Delhi for Jats; while in the more backward districts, unaccustomed to military service, local depots were established for the training of the young recruits near their homes. Above all, assistance in raising men for the Army was made a duty of all executive and village officials and of all who were enjoying grants of land or other marks of consideration from Government, and one of the main qualifications in establishing claims on Government.[16] In each district, a War League or Recruiting Board was formed with Deputy Commissioner as president, a few leading officials and a large number of influential non-officials as members, to help in distributing and raising the quota proposed for the district.'[17]

Besides the people of the Punjab were put to numerous hazards in their economic and social life. Such hazards were quite glaring in the curtailment of facilities of travelling and of import and export of merchandise in the province. Nature too proved very cruel to the people. The heavy rains in the autumn of 1917 had caused the worst outbreak of malaria since 1908. The death toll was very heavy, and an enormous number of young men escaped only with their 'spleens so enlarged that they were rendered unfit for the army'. These misfortunes were utterly eclipsed by the terrible scourge of influenza which raged throughout the Punjab for about three months preceding the armistice. 'The people died like flies, the villages were harder hit than the towns, the men than women, and those in the prime of life worst of all. Whole families were wiped out by the dozens; the losses in most districts ran into tens of thousands. Altogether more than a million died in the Province, including the Indian States. Of these, more than two lakhs were men of military age.'[18]

The new Income-Tax Act and the more searching methods of enquiry in relation thereto as well as the interference with trade conditions had made the trading community restless. A circular was issued by the Punjab government making suggestions for obtaining contributions which could only be given effect to by using more than normal pressure. A part of the circular may be stated here. I am to suggest that Deputy Commissioners might assist in the campaign by estimating the contributions that might reasonably be expected from the various towns. In doing so they will derive such assurance from the local tax returns, especially where the assessments have recently been revised by the special establishment. Income-tax returns furnish, too, a fairly reliable index to the relative financial condition of individuals who are expected to help the loan and a rough standard, which it is believed is already being applied in some districts. To judge of the adequacy of their investments in it, it would not be unreasonable to expect that on an average an assessee would be in a position to invest in the War Loan from half to one-fourth of the income on which he is actually assessed. Applying this rough test or others, which may be found suitable to local conditions, Deputy Commissioners should be in a position to see whether towns and villages or individuals in their jurisdiction are doing what is expected of them.

'The Deputy Commissioner should then, by special meetings, formation of local committee of Sahukars and such expedients, endeavour to obtain the estimated sum as a minimum contribution. Local committees of traders and others presided over in large towns by Judicial Officers. Extra Assistant Commissioners for Tahsildars, will probably be able to affect a satisfactory distribution of the loan demand. Rivalry between towns and communities might be promoted by periodical publication and comparison of the amounts subscribed. Help might be afforded by a promise to recognise liberal subscriptions by Sanads, by the grant of Chairs, and by the gift of Special certificates. On the other hand, it should be made clear to wealthy citizens that failure to do their duty in this matter will be taken into account in nominations to Municipal and notified area committees, in appointments of honorary magistrates and in any other forms of Government recognition, on the ground that such honours are reserved for those who have shown in a practical form their desire to assist the administration.'[19]

Besides, judicial processes were pressed into service. 'The first class magistrate at Chakwal discharged an accused in a criminal case No. 82 of 1917 noting that 'the accused and his brother have between them subscribed ₹ 110 towards "Our Day Fund", and according to verbal compromise made, accused is accordingly acquitted'. Mehar Singh, son of Daulat Singh, applied for remission of income tax in case No. 36 of 1917 in the same court. The magistrate in dismissing the application remarked among other things, 'owing to the war, the profit of the mules is immense, but the objector has not contributed a piece to any war fund or any war loan. He has also a son whom he would not enlist.'[20]

At Leiah, in the district of Muzaffargarh, a large crowd besieged the residence of the Naib Tahsildar, assaulted his peon and a policeman. Some persons were arrested and were tried under section 147 of the Indian Penal Code. On appeal, the judge remarked that 'the people had real grievances for which they wanted to find expression. It is a matter of common knowledge that the efforts of the subordinate officials in Muzaffargarh to raise the war loan and to find recruits, owing to the methods adopted by *Zaildars* and *Lambardars* on whom pressure was brought to help in the matter, led to severe friction in many places. It must be admitted too that these methods were frequently unauthorised, objectionable, oppressive, and opposed to the intentions of the Government. In remote tracts, they were found intolerable by the people. These acts could not, of course, be proved by the prosecution, and it would be absurd to expect proof of them to be adduced in defence in a case of the present kind. It is necessary in the cause of justice to make this clear, even if in doing so I have to get outside the judicial record.'[21]

Besides, many important cities and towns of the Punjab, viz., Lahore, Amritsar, Gujranwala, Wazirabad, Kasur, Akalgarh, Hafizabad, Patti and Khem Karan came under the special income-tax scheme of the Government and this increase was very large, ranging from 100 to 200 per cent.[22] The seizure of wheat-stocks under the Defence of India Act to step speculation and reduce the price of grain to the poor was also disliked by the traders affected thereby.[23]

The unrest spread like wildfire in the rural areas where peasantry had numerous grievances against the policy of the Government. The apathy of the governmental policy towards them and the utter neglect of their basic needs had greatly agitated their minds. They indeed had lost all hopes of their future progress, if any, from the functioning of the alien government.

At this point of time Gandhi stated: 'Tales of rank injustice and oppression came pouring in daily from the Punjab, but all I could do was to sit helplessly by and quash my teeth.'[24] Indeed the emergence of Gandhi on the political scene of India afforded a new kind of awakening to the Indian masses who heeded a leader with a firm resolve and determination to lead them and show them the way towards the cherished goal.[25] With the sudden demise of two political stalwarts, Gopal Krishna Gokhale and Pherozeshah Mehta in 1915, the moderates were in a state of depression, Bal Gangadhar Tilak, after his release, was not in the mainstream of the Indian National Congress. He was constantly shadowed by the intelligence department. Even bureaucracy was his sworn enemy.

Gandhi thought it as an act of farsightedness not to embarrass the British Government during the war. Probably, by doing so, he wished to demonstrate that he was no opportunist, taking advantage of the critical situation of the time. But he, however, gave vent to his feelings thus:[26] 'I feel sure that nothing less than a definite vision of Home Rule to be realised in the shortest possible time will satisfy the Indian people. Ours is a peculiar position. We are today outside the partnership. Ours is a consecration based on the hope of a better future. I should be untrue to you and to my country if I do not clearly and unequivocally tell you what that hope is. I do not bargain for its fulfilment, but you should know disappointment of hope means disillusion.'

The year 1916 was unique in the history of Indian nationalism in numerous ways, whereas it led to the foundation of two Home Rule Leagues with the same kinds of political programme, it brought all kinds of political differences and controversies to an end and set the stage in a smooth way for the emancipation of India.[27] This kind of model brought about Hindu-Muslim unity and formulated a mutually agreed conjoint scheme of self-government for the country to be placed before the government. No less significant was the reunion of the two wings of the Indian National Congress which had separated at Surat about nine years ago. The leadership of the Congress followed up the scheme of self-government by a resolution calling upon its various committees and other organised bodies and associations to carry on propaganda campaign in its favour throughout the country and educated public opinion on the issue.

The commencement of year 1917 witnessed a quickening of national consciousness all over the country and a widely popular agitation in favour of self-government. As prominent leaders of the Home Rule Movement, Tilak and Annie Besant did marvellous work and gained much prominence in politics in a short time. Tilak exhorted the people to insist on the demand of their rights: 'India is your own house. Our domestic affairs must be in our own hands. Freedom is my birthright. So long as it is awake within me, I am not old. No weapon can cut this spirit, no fire can burn it, no wind can dry it . . . We ask for Home Rule and we must get it.'[28]

The provincial leaders of all schools of thought like Motilal Nehru, Tej Bahadur Sapru, C.R. Das, C.P. Ramaswami Aiyar, M.A. Jinnah, Bhulabhai Desai, M.R. Jayakar and others joined the Home Rule League to spite the British government. When Annie Besant was served with the order of internment by the Governor of Madras in 1917, there was angry uproar and much excitement against the order, and her movement progressed in a geometrical progression.[29]

These unexpected political developments opened the eyes of the British statesmen to the realities of the prevailing situation which created an unfavourable atmosphere not congenial for the smooth and proper functioning of the governmental machinery at various levels. The Hindu-Muslim concord, the Lucknow

Pact, the reunion of the moderates and the extremists and the intensive and extensive propaganda for Home Rule could not be ignored, rather they were taken up with all seriousness. Austin Chamberlain suggested to the British cabinet to take practical steps to meet the powerful and increasing- demand of the united India for greater share of its people in the administration of the country, but cautioned against making the constitutional changes appear as rewards for services rendered by India in the war.

With the approval of the war cabinet[30] headed by Lloyd George, E.S. Montagu, the Secretary of State for India, made an historic declaration on 20 August, 1917: 'The policy of His Majesty's Government, with which the Government of India are in complete accord, is that of the increasing association of Indians in every branch of the administration and the gradual development of self-governing institutions with a view to the progressive realization of responsible Government in India as an integral part of the British Empire. . . I would add that progress in this policy can only be achieved by successive stages. The British Government and the Government of India, on whom the responsibility lies for the welfare and advancement of the Indian people, must be the judges of the time and measure of each advance, and they must be guided by the co-operation received from those upon whom new opportunities of service will thus be conferred and by the extent to which it is found that confidence can be reposed in their sense of responsibility.'[31]

The conclusion of the First World War had also brought forward the complex and ticklish problems emanating from the terms on which peace was to be concluded with Turkey, a dismembered empire by the Allied Powers. The Muslims in India became much apprehensive and unhappy with the policy of the British government over the question of Khilafat which had deep religious sanctity for them and touched upon their sentiments when the treatment of the British government with the Caliph and his territories were explained and discussed both by the Muslim and Hindu leadership.

During the year 1918, the tension between the government and prominent leaders of the Congress grew mainly due to their speeches and tours in various regions. Early in 1918, Bal Gangadhar Tilak and Bipin Chandra Pal were prohibited from entering Delhi and the Punjab. The Punjab government felt panicky about the outbreak of an organised rebellion by the people and this state of panic was greatly responsible for the inhuman brutalities committed by the government later.[32]

The Secretary of State who was indeed very meticulous in maintaining a diary, with day-to-day record, happened to come to India after about three months of his announcement and toured a major portion of the country in a period of six months till he left for England in May 1918. He recorded thus: 'My visit to India means that we are going to do something big. I cannot go home and produce a little thing or nothing, it must be epoch-making or it is a failure, it must be the keynote of the future history of India.'[33]

Undoubtedly, India had nobly supported the Empire in its war against Germany. Its teeming millions had contributed to the war effort in both money and men and for the common cause they had endured the hardships of food scarcity, rising prices, increased taxation, the restriction of press freedom and the curtailment of personal liberty without complaint. They had been stricken by severe famine on the failure of the monsoon in 1918 and had suffered terrible mortality from the world-wide influenza epidemic of that year. The armistice found them restless and excited. They were stirred by the new spirit of personal freedom and national liberty brought to the surface throughout the world by war. They were intoxicated by the new conception of the self-determination of peoples voiced by President Wilson of the United States, and agitated by the Bolshevik Revolution of 1917 which they saw as the triumph of the oppressed. The people of India, goaded by the ferment of the time, thought that a new dawn was breaking. Reforms had been promised by the Imperial Government, their goal and Home Rule, by successive stages. Great expectations had been raised. The people of India felt that they had helped to win the war, now was the time for their reward. They had proved their right to be treated as an equal member of the Empire.

'The White Sahibs, who had governed India since the days of the Mutiny when the rule of the East India Company had been ended, failed to understand the strength of Indian hopes of self-government.'[34]

Jawaharlal Nehru recorded in his *Autobiography* thus: 'The end 'of the World War found India in a state of suppressed excitement. Industrialisation had spread and the capitalist class had grown in wealth and power. This handful at the top had prospered and were greedy for more power and opportunity to invest their savings and add to their wealth. The great majority, however, were not so fortunate and looked forward to a lightening of the burdens that crushed them.'[33]

Michael O'Dwyer was a firm believer in strong-arm methods and made no secret of his views for political reforms demanded by the Congress leadership. He gave a severe warning to the press which was followed by action under the Press Act. Security was demanded and forfeited in a number of cases. He even prevented the entry of newspapers like *New India*, *Amrita Bazar Patrika* and *Independent* into the Punjab. Annie Besant wrote, 'The harsh oppressive rule of Sir Michael O'Dwyer, his press-gang methods of recruitment, his forced war-loans and his cruel persecution of all political leaders kept the covered-up members of resentment alive and ready to break into flame.'

'The attitude of the Government of India and the British non-official community had greatly hardened against the more radical section of the Congress since the partition of Bengal. The Government tended to identify the extremists with the terrorists. But stern coercive measures instead of curbing the terrorists had the effect of sending them underground inside India and promoting armed intervention from abroad.'[36]

The administration of the Punjab government under Michael O'Dwyer had for various reasons come to be regarded by the educated and politically-minded classes as opposed to their patriotic and nationalist sentiments and aspirations. Moreover, during his term of office orders had been issued prohibiting prominent politicians from entering the Punjab and reports of the proceedings of certain meetings had been prohibited publication unless they had been censored. He had objected to Tej Bahadur Sapru and Pandit Madan Mohan Malaviya being invited to attend the conference that was held at Lahore to support the reforms proposals of the nineteen members of the Indian Legislative Council. The Defence of India Act was passed as an emergency measure to cope with revolutionary outbreaks that were feared during the war. 'It is possible to understand the use of such powers when all available fighting material had been removed from India to the battlefields of France and Mesopotamia, and when India's internal peace had to depend largely upon the loyalty and the peace-loving nature of the people. Extraordinary powers taken by the Executive, like martial law, enable one policeman to do the work of perhaps four, but this is done at the cost of the liberty of the subject, by depriving him of all the wholesome checks which regulate police procedure. When, therefore, the hostilities ceased, the people had looked forward to the repeal of the Defence of India Act. They had done so the more because, in spite of the declarations made by the Government that the measure would be used only in case of real necessity and never for the purpose of stifling political agitation or hindering the movements of public men, it was used for the purpose of restraining political freedom. To mention no other case it was used in order to intern Mrs. Besant and her associates because they represented in its intense form the Indian Home Rule movement. In it, there never was any suspicion of violence entertained even by her worst enemies. The public had, therefore, grown thoroughly distrustful of the Government, and had hoped that in view of India's unique war record, and the declaration of August 1917 foreshadowing reforms leading to responsible Government, that Act would be repealed and that the people would have respite from the unwelcome attentions of the Secret Service Department.'

Thus Michael O'Dwyer galvanized the Punjab into life and made the Punjabis feel akin in a manner, they had never done before. He made a 'supreme effort' to crush the spirit of the people that was struggling with all sincerity to be free from the thraldom under which he had bound it under his rule. He scented danger in every honest and patriotic speech made by the leaders and he detected conspiracy in every kind of gathering, association and combination. By the application of illegal and harsh methods to silence the feelings of the people, he instead invited violence from them so that he might justify the use of force to crush them through the agency of civilian bureaucracy at tahsil, district and divisional levels as well as with the support of the loyal and picked officials of the defence services. This kind of policy, however, succeeded as a temporary phase to establish law and order in various areas, but its aftermath effects reached such a climax that it became difficult for the British government to have a firm grip over the political situation engineered and led by no less a person than Mahatma Gandhi who was instrumental in having a huge following within the Congress-fold throughout India and managing the mass support for the first Non-Cooperation Movement launched in 1920.

REFERENCES

1. For details see Hugh Johnston, *The Voyage of the Komagata Maru: The Sikh Challenge to Canada's Colour Bar*, Delhi, 1979, pp. 15 ff.
2. *Ibid.*, pp. 113-15.
3. S.R. Bakshi, *Bhagat Singh and His Ideology*, Delhi, 1981, see the Introduction.
4. Hanson W. Baldwin, *World War I*, London, 1963, pp. 19 ff.
5. He was appointed the Lieutenant-Governor of Punjab in 1913.
6. Michael O'Dwyer, *India As I Knew It*, London, 1925, p. 217.
7. *Ibid.*, p. 419.
8. V.N. Datta, *Jallianwala Bagh*, Ludhiana, 1969, pp. 12-13.
9. *Ibid.*, p. 13.
10. Michael O'Dwyer, *op. cit.*, pp. 225-26.
11. M.S. Leigh, *The Punjab and the War*, Lahore, 1922, p. 41.
12. K. Antonova, G. Bongard-Levin and G. Kotovsky, *A History of India*, Vol. II, Moscow, 1978, pp. 143-44.
13. M.S. Leigh, *op. cit.*, pp. 13-14.
14. Michael O'Dwyer, *op. cit.*, pp. 218 ff.
15. *Ibid.*
16. *Ibid.*
17. *Ibid.*

18. M.S. Leigh, *op. cit.,* p. 11.
19. Report of the Commission appointed by the Punjab Sub-Committee of the Indian National Congress, Bombay, 1920, p. 17.
20. *Ibid.,* pp. 17-18.
21. *Ibid.,* p. 18.
22. *Disorders Inquiry Committee Report, 1919-20*, Calcutta, 1920, p. 152.
23. *Ibid.*
24. M.K. Gandhi, *The Story of My Experiments with Truth*, Ahmedabad, 1929, p. 516.
25. Louis Fischer, *The Life of Mahatma Gandhi,* London, 1962, pp. 141 ff.
26. M.K. Gandhi, *op. cit.,* pp. 273-74,
27. *Speeches and Writings of Annie Besant*, Madras, n.d., pp. 33 ff.
28. *Bal Gangadhar Tilak, His Writings and Speeches*, Madras, n.d., pp. 230 ff.
29. *Speeches and Writings of Annie Besant*, Madras, n.d. p. 41.
30. The other prominent members of the Coalition Government were E.S. Montagu, Lord Curzon, Lord Milner and Balfour.
31. Report on Indian Constitutional Reforms, 1918, p. 1.
32. D.P. Mishra, *The History of Freedom Movement in Madhya Pradesh*, Nagpur, 1956, p. 280.
33. E.S. Montagu, *An Indian Diary,* London, 1930, p. 8.
34. Rupert Furneaux, *Massacre at Amritsar,* London, 1963, pp. 33-34.
35. Jawaharlal Nehru, *An Autobiography,* Delhi, 1962, p. 40.
36. Tara Chand, *History of the Freedom Movement in India*, Vol. III, 1972, p. 471.

Chapter 2
Repressive Laws

When the First World War ended, the people were looking forward to the repeal of the Defence of India Act. They had begun to detest this Act, because contrary to the government's declaration, it was used by Michael O'Dwyer to punish people of the Punjab and suppress their political aspirations. Indeed, there had been a promise by the British government in August 1917 of advance towards responsible government and people had begun hoping that the Defence of India Act would soon be repealed and they would have some respite from the 'unwelcome and unwanted' attentions of the secret service department.

The Rowlatt Bills came as a surprise as they were sprung upon an indignant, angry and dissatisfied people. These Bills take their popular name from the president of the Sedition Committee. This Committee was appointed by the government of India on 10 December, 1917 with Mr. Justice Rowlatt as president to report on what were termed as 'criminal conspiracies connected with revolutionary movements in India', and advise about legislation to deal with them. The committee was required to sit in camera. Its report was presented on 15 April, 1918.

The committee prepared a fairly detailed account of the organization and doings of young revolutionaries operating in different regions of India. This was done mainly on the basis of material supplied by the government of India. After a comprehensive survey of the existing political situation, the committee recommended special legislation which sought to curtail the liberty and legal rights of the people in a manner very drastic in nature. Consequently, two Bills were prepared on the basis of these recommendations. The one that actually passed into law, was the Anarchical and Revolutionary Crimes Act, 1919. It made provision for speedy trial of officers by a Special Court, consisting of three High Court judges. There could be no appeal against decisions of this court and the provincial government was empowered to search a place and arrest a suspected person without warrant and keep him in confinement at any place in the country.

The police had no knowledge of the nature of the evidence given before the committee or even the names of those who gave it. The witnesses were not cross-examined on behalf of the people who were unrepresented. In spite of the passionate protest, the Bill was rushed through, and during all the crucial stages of the voting, no Indian member of the Legislative Council voted in any manner in its favour except one member of the Executive Council and he, too, was to resign soon afterwards after having witnessed the consequences in Punjab. The Bill was finally passed on 18 March, 191A and three important members of the Imperial Legislative Council, M.M. Malaviya, M.A. Jinnah and Mazharul Haque resigned.

Jinnah, the chairman of the Muslim League, warned the government, in his speech in the Assembly, 'I do not wish to state it by way of threat or intimidation to Government, but I wish to state it because it is my duty to tell you that, if these measures are passed, you will create in the country from one end to the other a discontent and agitation, the like of which you have not witnessed, and it will have, believe me, a most disastrous effect on the good relations that have existed between the Government and people.'[1] In his letter of resignation to the Viceroy, he stated: 'The Government of India and Your Excellency have thought it fit to place on the Statute Book a measure admittedly obnoxious and decidedly coercive at a time of peace and thereby substituted the Executive for the Judicial. Besides, by passing this Bill Your Excellency's Government have actively negatived every argument they advanced but an year ago, when they appealed to India for help at the War Conference and ruthlessly trampled upon the principles for which Great Britain avowedly fought the war. The fundamental principles of justice have been violated at a time when there is no real danger to the State ... In my opinion a Government that passes or sanctions such a law in times of peace forfeits its claim to be called a civilized Government.'[2]

The Bill was strenuously opposed throughout the country by Indians of all shades of opinion. As could be anticipated, the Bill was criticised in numerous public meetings. The significant point of criticism was that the British Government did not care to realize the true impact of the situation from the point of view of nationalist India.

P.E. Richards in his work on *Indian Dust* mentioned thus on 14 April, 1919: "Lahore is in the possession of armed police and British troops. Women and children have been ordered to leave the Hill stations . . . The colleges have joined in the strike ... At all the important points were British khaki and machine-guns.'[3]

Several Indian newspapers levelled severe criticism against this Bill. The *Bombay Chronicle* called it as 'repression in excelsis'.[4] The *Hindu* wrote, '. . . the Indian public would read the proposed provisions with shame, indignation and disgust'.[5] The *Amrita Bazar Patrika* called it a 'gigantic blunder which would arouse the worst passions of a peaceful law-abiding people.'[9] The *Panjabee* regarded it as 'a bare-faced attempt on the part of a bureaucracy which has been demoralised by the exercise of unrestrained power to interfere with liberty.'[7] The *New India* described it as 'monstrous'.[8]

The speedy trials were to be conducted without any kind of commitment and with no right to appeal. They could take place *in camera*. Besides, the relevant provisions of the Criminal Procedure Code and the Evidence Act were superseded for purposes of this legislation. The preventive powers were conferred on the authorities; this included the taking of security from ordinary people, and the insistence on their giving an undertaking that they would not commit a scheduled offence, that they would not change residence without notice, and that they would report to the nearest police station from time to time. The authorities were given power to use all means to enforce compliance. The people affected would have no right of counsel in their pleadings. In short, as the Congress Enquiry

Report said, 'The Act created licentious conditions of judicial administration.' The Report added that the provisions for arrest without warrant and confinement under all sorts of conditions meant organised terror and disorder, martial law without the name. There were indeed shouts everywhere, *'No Appeal, No Dalil, No Vakil.*"

'One could ask why this was at all necessary. Did not Government have in its possession all the law that was required—the Defence of India Act, the Press Act, the Criminal Procedure Amendment Act and the time-worn 1818 Regulations? . . . The only purpose that the appointment of the committee served was to provoke and exasperate the people. They saw in it the beginning of another era of repression. It was as if Government wished to forestall any feeling of exultation among the people as a result of the Parliamentary Declaration of 20th August. It was a warning that more diabolical weapons were being sharpened for the chastisement of the so-called sedition-mongers. Once again the bureaucracy had successfully queered the pitch for any peaceful progress."[9]

On 8 February, 1919, Gandhi informed Madan Mohan Malaviya of his reaction about the Rowlatt Bills. 'The Viceroy's speech is disappointing. Under the circumstances I, at any rate, hope that all the Indian members will leave the Select Committee or, if necessary, even the Council, and launch a countrywide agitation. You and other members have said that if the Rowlatt Bills are passed a massive agitation would be launched the like of which has not been seen in India ... I have not yet fully decided but I feel that when the Government bring in an obnoxious law the people will be entitled to defy their other laws as well. If we do not show the strength of the people, even the reforms we are to get will be useless. In my opinion you should all make it clear to the Government that so long as the Rowlatt Bills are there you will pay no taxes and will advise the people also not to pay them. I know that to give such advice is to assume a great responsibility. But unless we do something really big they will not feel any respect for us. And we cannot hope to get anything from people who do not respect us.'[10]

The next day, Gandhi communicated to V.S. Srinivasa Sastri that he could no longer watch the progress of the Rowlatt Bills as they were the aggravated symptoms of the deep-seated disease. For him, they were a striking demonstration of the determination of the council service 'to retain its grip of our necks'. He considered the Bills to be an open challenge to us and if 'we succumb we are done for.' He clarified, 'When petitions and resolutions of gigantic mass meetings fail, there are but two courses open—the ordinary rough and ready course is an armed rebellion, and the second is civil disobedience to all the laws of the land or to a selection of them. If the Bills were but a stray example of lapse of righteousness and justice, I should not mind then but when they are clearly an evidence of a determined policy of repression, civil disobedience seems to be a duty imposed upon every lover of personal and public liberty.' Gandhi felt sure that the resignations of Indian members would shake the British Government's confidence in its ability to disregard public sentiment and thus would be no an education of immense value to the people of India.'[11]

J.B. Kripalani reacted thus: 'It was during these days that the World War ended. The allies were victorious. However, there was no evidence of any change in Britain's attitude towards India. In fact, it looked as though with the end of their pre-occupation with the war, they had decided to turn their attention to the danger of an awakened India. The Defence of India Act was still on the Statute Book. Even then the Rowlatt Committee was appointed to enquire into the nature of Indian unrest and suggest measures to meet its threat to the Empire.[12]

'But events were moving fast. Harrowing reports of the wanton violence that the Government was using on peaceful demonstrators were pouring in from all parts of the country, more especially from the Punjab. The repression evoked further demonstrations. In some places, these took a violent turn. Some British and Indian officers were killed. There were reports of rioting in Ahmedabad and other parts of Gujarat and in the Punjab. Gandhiji rushed to Ahmedabad. When he learnt that his followers, who had pledged themselves to non-violence, had yielded to the provocation given by the authorities, he was greatly distressed. *Satyagraha* required strict adherence to nonviolence even under the severest provocation. Gandhiji felt that people had not grasped the full meaning of his message. They were not yet ready to use the new weapon of non-violence. He, therefore, called off the movement and admitted that he had made 'a Himalayan miscalculation' inasmuch as he had overrated the patience of the people and their capacity for disciplined action.'[13]

Srinivasa Sastri remarked, 'A bad law once passed is not always used against the bad. . . In times of panic caused, it may be, by very slight incidents, I have known Governments lose their heads. I have known a reign of terror being brought about. I have known the best, the noblest Indians, the highest characters amongst us, brought under suspicion, standing in hourly dread of the visitations of the Criminal Investigation Department . . . When Government undertakes a repressive policy, the innocent are not safe. Men like me would not be considered innocent. The innocent then is he who foreswears politics, who takes no part in the public movements of the times; who retires into his house, mumbles his prayers, pays his taxes, and *salams* all the government officials allround. The man who interferes in politics, the man who goes about collecting money for any public purpose, the man who addresses a public meeting, then becomes a suspect. . . . You may enlarge your councils, you may advise wide electorates, but the men that will then fill your councils will be toadies, timid men and the bureaucracy, armed with these repressive powers, will reign unchecked under the outward forms of a democratic government. Well, we are all anxious to punish the wicked. None of us desire that wickedness should go unpunished but. . . even the wicked must be punished in certain ways. When Skeffington was shot, I remember the whole world was shocked . . . Now in war, when all humanity throbs with excitement and peril, and nobody thinks of anything except how to conquer the enemy, even then, my Lord, there are criminals abroad in a country, there are certain ways in which they ought to be brought to book. You ought not to lay them by the heels and punish them in ways that will shock the sense of justice; in ways that will make the innocent feel that there is no law in the land; in ways that will make honest, virtuous and public spirited work impossible. The price even for the extinction of wickedness that is demanded then is far too high. . . Much better that a few rascals should walk abroad, than that the honest man should be obliged for fear of the law of the land to remain shut up in his house, to refrain from the activities which it is in his nature to indulge in, to abstain from all political and public work merely because there is a dreadful law in the land.'

Sastri was not in agreement with William Vincent's dictum that the aim of the Bill, he was in-charge of, was not 'the suppression but the purification of politics'. He remarked— 'The history of legislation, both social and political, is strewn with instances of miscarriage of excellent intentions. Laws intended to cure poverty have aggravated it . . . You cannot place on the Statute Book such drastic legislation without putting into the hands of overenthusiastic executive officers what I consider short-cuts to administrative peace . . . The tragic story of India may be summed up in these words, that you have governed all the centuries in India in isolation, without having any responsible section of public opinion behind you . . . No section of public opinion supports you. The nominated members have not given their blessing to this Bill. The Zamindar members have not given their blessing. The lawyer members will have none of it. The members of commerce will have none of it . . .'

'. . . I do not think the Hon'ble the Law Member could have meant all that he said that some of us were indulging in threat of agitation, I venture to think that no one here who has spoken against the Bill indulged in any thing which might truthfully be described as a threat of agitation. None of us, certainly none of the Moderates. I take leave to say, have power to go and stir up a violent agitation in the country. It is impossible. Agitation must be there already. The heart must be throbbing, if any words that we use here can have a possible effect on the general political atmosphere. The agitation is there. I wish to assure my official colleagues that none of us has a share yet in this business, but, if our appeals fall flat, if the Bill goes through, I do not believe there is any one who would be doing his duty if he did not join the agitation.'

In spite, however, of the serious protest, the motion that the Bill be referred to a Select Committee, was carried, and the amendment, that its consideration be deferred till six months after the term of office of the Legislative Council, was defeated on 6 February, 1919; 22 voted for the amendment and 35 against it.

Ayes 22

Gangadhar Chitnavis, S.N. Banerjea, Raja of Mahmudabad, Tej Bahadur Sapru, Madan Mohan Malaviya, Srinivasa Sastri, B.N. Sharma, Mir Asad Ali, V.J. Patel, M.A. Jinnah, Fazalbhoy Currimbhoy, Sitanath Roy, Rampal Singh, Krishna Sahay, Raja of Nanika, Mazharul Haque, Mian Muhammad Shafi, Zulfikar Ali Khan, G.S. Khaparde, B.D. Shukul, K.K. Chanda, and Maung Bah Too.

Noes 35

H.E. the Commander-in-Chief of India, Claude Hill, Sankaran Nair, George Lowndes, William Vincent, James Meston, Arthur Anderson, W.A. Ironside, Verney Lovett, H.F. Howard, James Du Boulay, A.H. Ley, H. Sharp, R.A. Mant, Alfred Bingley, Godfrey Fell, F.C. Rose, C.H. Kesteve, D. de S. Bray R.E. Holland, W.R. Edwards, G.R. Clarke, A.P. Muddiman, C.A. Barron, P.L. Moore, M.N. Hogg, T. Emerson, E.H.C. Walsh, C.A. Kincaid, John Donald, P.J. Fagan, J.T. Marten. W.J. Reid, W.F. Pice and H. Moncrieff Smith.

Jawaharlal Nehru opined thus: 'It was proposed in the initial stages that this Act, when passed, was to be a permanent measure, but an amendment was accepted in the select committee limiting its continuance to three years from the termination of the war . . . the British Government, in the teeth of unanimous public opinion, pushed through a law which they themselves never used afterwards, and thus invited an upheaval. One might almost think that the object of the measure was to bring trouble.'[14]

The passage of the Rowlatt Bills in the final shape of an Act raised a storm and a huge and massive opposition unprecedented in the history of India. 'The crime of the Government became complete when they persisted in it in the face of unanimous popular opposition: The Government were wholly unjustified in placing on the Statute Book, on the eve of liberal reforms, an extraordinary measure to deal with anarchy, as if anarchy had been endemic instead of being rare in India.' Whatever the object of the Rowlatt Bills, the provisions were so drastic that the people of India began to feel that their freedom was in peril.

The response to Gandhi's call for satyagraha was spontaneous and phenomenal. His message for the people of India reached the four corners of the country even though the Congress organisation had not become so strong and widespread. On 24 Feb, 1919, a *Satyagraha Pledge*[15] under the signatures of Gandhi, Vallabhbhai Patel, Chandulal Manilal Desai, Anasuya Sarabhai and others was issued as a protest against the Bills. 'Being conscientiously of opinion that the Bills known as the Indian Criminal Law (Amendment) Bill, No. I of 1919 and the Criminal Law (Emergency Powers) Bill. No. II of 1919 are unjust, subversive of the principle of liberty and justice, and destructive of the elementary rights of individuals on which the safety of the community as a whole and the State itself is based, we solemnly affirm that, in the event of these Bills becoming law and until they are withdrawn, we shall refuse civilly to obey the laws and such other laws as a Committee to be hereafter appointed may think fit and we further affirm that in this struggle we will faithfully follow truth and refrain from violence to life, person or property.'[19]

On the same day, Gandhi sent a telegram to the Private Secretary to the Viceroy in which he expressed his sentiments about the Rowlatt Bills. 'Ever since publication Rowlatt Bills have been considering my position regarding them. Have been conferring with friends. In my opinion bad in themselves Bills are but symptoms of deep-seated disease among the ruling class, coming as they do on eve reforms Bills augur ill for their success. Those who have been associated with me in public work and other friends met today and after the greatest deliberation have decided to offer *satyagraha* and commit civil disobedience of such laws as committee to be formed from ourselves may decide. After Sir George Lowndes' speech it is necessary to demonstrate to Government that even a Government the most autocratic finally owes its power to the will of the Government. Without recognition of this principle and consequently withdrawal of Bills many of us consider reforms valueless. I wish to make a humble but strong appeal to His Excellency to reconsider Government's decision to proceed with Bills, and reluctantly and that in event of unfavourable reply to the pledge must be published and the signatures must invite additions. I am aware of seriousness of the proposed step. It is, however, much better that people say openly what they think in their hearts and without fear of consequences enforce the dictates of their own conscience. May I expect early reply?[17]

On 26 February, the Congress leadership issued instructions to the *satyagraha* volunteers to be carried on by them while seeking support of the people for the national cause. Volunteers were required to read and explain the *Satyagraha Pledge* to every intending signatory before taking his signature to the vow for the national cause. The pledge was in three parts. The first part laid down the aims and objects of the pledge. It declared that the signatories were of opinion that the Rowlatt Bills were unjust, subversive of the principle of liberty and justice, and destructive of the elementary rights of individuals. In order to be able to make this statement one must fully understand the Rowlatt Bills, hence it was the duty of the volunteers to explain the Bills clearly to the intending signatory.[18]

The exact vow to be taken by the *satyagraha* volunteers formed the second part of the pledge. The signatory had to solemnly affirm that he would refuse civilly to disobey certain laws. 'Volunteers must explain to the signatory the full significance of the word 'civilly' . . . the possession and distribution to the public of literature proscribed by Government and which one sincerely believes to be harmless, would be civil disobedience. Volunteers must explain to the would-be-signatory with the help of such illustrations the full significance of the pledge.'[19]

Besides volunteers were required to explain to every intending signatory that he must be prepared to bear every kind of suffering and to sacrifice, if necessary, both his person and property. He was also made to understand that he must be prepared to carry on the struggle single-handed even if left alone.[20]

The third part of the pledge declared that the *satyagrahi* would fearlessly adhere to the principles of truth and *ahimsa*. He must not misrepresent anything or hurt anybody's feelings. Volunteers must urge upon people necessity of fully realizing the grave responsibility of adhering to truth and *ahimsa* before signing the pledge. Volunteer must not speak of things they did not understand and must not hold out false hopes to anybody.[21] If they found themselves unable to explain anything they must consult the committee or refer the would-be signatory to it. *Ahimsa* included *advesha*. Volunteers, therefore, must never resort to unfair criticism of the movement.[22] If in performing their duties they were obstructed by the police or others, they must not lose their temper but must courteously explain to those opposing them, their (volunteers') duty and their determination under any circumstances to perform the same.[23]

Volunteers were to accept the signatures of persons under eighteen and also students. And even in the case of those over 18, he must make sure that the signatory had decided after careful consideration. But volunteers must not induce persons to sign, upon whose earnings their families were solely dependent for their maintenance.[24]

Gandhi started the *Satyagraha Sabha,* the members of which were pledged to disobey the Rowlatt Act, if it was applied to them, as well as other objectionable laws to be specified from time to time. In other words they were to court gaol openly and deliberately. Jawaharlal Nehru reacted thus: 'When I first read about this proposal in the newspapers my reaction was one of tremendous relief. Here at last was a way out of the tangle, a method of action which was straight and open and possibly effective, I was afire with enthusiasm and wanted to join the *Satyagraha Sabha* immediately. I hardly thought of the consequences—law-breaking, gaol-going, etc., and if I thought of them I did not care.'[25]

On 11 March, Gandhi once again reminded the Viceroy of the serious repercussions the passage of Rowlatt Bills would lead to in the country. In a telegram to him, he explained, 'Even at this eleventh hour I respectfully ask His Excellency and his Government to pause and consider before passing Rowlatt Bills. Whether justified or not, there is no mistaking the strength of public opinion on the measures. I am sure Government do not intend intensifying existing bitterness. Government will risk nothing by delay, but by expressly bowing to public opinion will smooth down feeling and enhance real prestige. I am proceeding to Bombay tomorrow by Jubbulpore Mail.'[26]

The passing of the Act through the Legislative Council had resulted in the vernacular presses of Delhi indulging in extravagant language and there had been meetings in Delhi condemning the Act. On 30th March, rioting which was the outcome of the *hartal* and so-called passive resistance, took place. The crowds in the city were disorderly—mainly in the Chandni Chowk and Hauz Kazi and people were being prevented from riding in *tongas* by the mob. 'It appears that a mob of people presumably some of those who had been enforcing *hartal* and stopping vehicles had invaded the Railway Station with the object of closing down the shops of the station, sweetmeat vendors who supply passengers with food and refreshment. A European had been pulled out of a *tonga* and the driver was assaulted and the precincts of the Railway Station were the scene of more disorderly conduct. At least one man was arrested by the Railway police.

. . . Mr. Mathews, the Assistant Station Superintendent was assaulted, his coat being torn off his back. A very excited crowd of rowdies invaded the Railway Station breaking flowerpots and damaging railway property.

They however, created disturbance in the station yard and in the road with the object of releasing men whom they imagined had been arrested. . . . The police drove the crowd off and into the Queen's Gardens opposite, and both police and troops were utilised to prevent the crowd returning to the station.

The upshot was that crowd became more and more unruly and excited, and proceeded to attack the forces present with sticks and stones. Matters came to such a pass that for the protection of the troops and police, many of whom had been hit including Mr. Marshall, Mr. Jeffreys, Sergeant Kemsley and even Mr. Currie himself. Mr. Currie sanctioned fire being opened, both police and troops firing a few rounds. As soon as the crowd began to withdraw, the order to cease fire was issued. Two rioters were killed inside the Queen's Gardens, and doubtless more were wounded.[27]

Initially, 30th March 1919 was fixed for the national protest, but the date was changed to 6th April. It was a simple, yet unique programme of mass action—24-hour fast as a necessary discipline, the stopping of all work, the closing of all markets and business places and the holding of public meetings.[28]

On 7 April, 1919, Gandhi launched a daily entitled *Satyagrahi* in defiance of the Indian Press Act. The paper had not been registered in accordance with the law. Gandhi explained to the subscribers: 'So there can be no annual subscription. Nor can it be guaranteed that the paper will be published without interruption. The editor (M.K. Gandhi) is liable at any moment to be arrested by the Government and it is impossible to ensure continuity of sublimation until India is in the happy position of supplying editors enough to take the place of these arrested. We shall leave no stone unturned to secure a ceaseless succession of editors. It is not our intention to break for all time the law governing publication of newspapers. This paper will, therefore, exist so long only as the Rowlatt legislation is not withdrawn.'[29]

In fact, *Satyagrahi* had come into being for the sake of ensuring withdrawal of the Rowlatt legislation. Its main motive, therefore, was to show to the people the ways and means of bringing about such withdrawal in accordance with the principles of *Satyagraha Pledge* required the signatories to court imprisonment by offering civil disobedience by committing a civil breach of certain laws. This publication can, therefore, show the best remedy in one way and that was by committing civil disobedience in the very act of publishing this journal. Thus this method of *Satyagraha* was unique. In it the example alone was precept. 'Therefore, whatever are suggested herein will be those that have been tested by personal experience, and remedies thus tested will be life well-tried medicine more valuable than new.'

A final guideline was issued by the *Satyagraha Sabha* to the *Satyagraha* volunteers on 7 April, 1919 along with a list of prohibited literature which should be made use of by them in public meetings. This prohibited literature was as follows:[30]

1. *Hind Swaraj* by M.K. Gandhi
2. *Sarvodaya or Universal Dawn* by M.K. Gandhi
3. *The Story of a Satyagrahi* by M.K. Gandhi
4. *The Life and Address of Mustafa Kamal Pasha*

In selecting this kind of prohibited literature, the *Satyagraha Sabha* had a few important considerations in view. Such a literature used by the *satyagrahis* was to cause as little disturbance as possible among the Governors and the governed. 'Until *satyagrahis* have become seasoned, disciplined and capable of handling delicately organized movements, to select such laws only as can be disobeyed individually; to select as a first step, laws that evoked popular disapproval and that from the *satyagraha* standpoint, are the most open to attack; to select laws whose civil breach would constitute an education for the people, showing them a clear way out of the difficulties that lie in the path of honest men desiring to do public work (and) regarding prohibited literature, to select such books and pamphlets as are not inconsistent with *satyagraha,* and which are, therefore, of a clean type which do not, either directly or indirectly, approve of or encourage violence.'[31]

Satyagraha volunteers were further advised to abide by some principles during the struggle. 'We are not in a position to expect to be arrested any moment. It is, therefore, necessary to bear in mind that, if anyone is arrested, he should without causing any difficulty allow himself to be arrested and, if summoned to appear before a court, he should do so. No defence should be offered and no pleaders engaged in the matter. If a fine is imposed with the alternative of imprisonment, imprisonment should be accepted. If only a fine is imposed, it ought not to be paid but that his property, if he has any, should be allowed to be sold. There should be no demonstration of grief or otherwise made by the remaining *satyagrahis* by reason of the arrest and imprisonment of their comrade. It cannot be too often repeated that we court imprisonment and we may not complain of it when we actually receive it. When once imprisoned, it is our duty to conform to all prison regulations, as prison reform is no part of our campaign at the present moment. A *satyagrahi* may not resort to surreptitious practices, of which ordinary prisoners are often found to be guilty. All a *satyagrahi* does can only and must be done openly.'[32]

The *satyagrahis* were advised to receive copies of prohibited literature for distribution amongst the people from the secretaries of the *Satyagraha Sabha.* A novel feature of such a distribution was that it was to be done not in a secret way. *Satyagrahis* were, therefore, required, as far as possible, to write their names and addresses as sellers, so that they might be traced without any kind of difficulty when they were wanted by the Government for prosecution, Naturally, there could be no question of secret sale of this literature.[33] It was open to *satyagrahis* to form small groups of men and women to whom they might read this class of literature. Thus the object in supplying the selected prohibited literature was not merely to commit a civil breach of the law regarding it, but it was also to provide people with clean literature of a high moral value. It was expected by the Congress leadership that the Government would confiscate such literature.[34]

Another unique feature of the *satyagraha* was that it was to be an independent of financial support as far as possible.[35] Moreover, when the copies of the prohibited literature were confiscated by the Government, *satyagrahis* were required to make more copies themselves or by securing the assistance of 'willing friends' and to make use of it until it was confiscated by giving readings to the people from it.[36] In fact, such readings would amount to dissemination of prohibited literature. When all the copies would exhaust by dissemination or confiscation, *satyagrahis* might continue civil disobedience by writing out and distributing extracts from accessible books.[37]

Regarding civil breach of the law governing publications of newspapers, the idea was to publish in every *satyagraha* centre a written newspaper, without registering it. It was not to occupy more than one side of half a foolscap. 'A *satyagrahi*, for whom punishments provided by law have lost all terror, can give only in an unregistered newspaper his thoughts and opinions unhampered by any other consideration than that of his own conscience. His newspaper, therefore, if otherwise well-edited, can become a most powerful vehicle for transmitting pure ideas in a concise manner, and there need be no fear of inability to circulate a hand-written newspaper; for it will be the duty of those why may receive the first copies to recopy till at last the process of multiplication is made to cover, if necessary, the whole of the masses of India. And it must not be forgotten that we have in India the tradition of imparting instructions by oral teaching.'[38]

A large number of protest meetings were organised in various parts of the country. The social discontent got wider circulation in Lahore, Amritsar, Delhi, Ahmedabad, Bombay, United Provinces, Central Provinces and Calcutta. The rural areas, except in the Punjab and Gujarat were not effected by this agitation. With the unchallenged charisma which indeed was an effective weapon in Gandhian political armoury, he brought about a drastic change in the existing climate of politics and could easily muster support from different sections of the community dwelling mainly in cities and larger towns. The effect of this agitation proved as a significant aspect for launching bigger movement at all-India level in 1920. Undoubtedly, the *satyagraha* was organised, guided and planned by Gandhi at higher level, but it was effectively supported by the local leaders with the local support. At times, the sentiments of the mobs crossed the non-violent domains and resorted to assault, arson, looting and killing. As a result thereof the Government machinery acted swiftly but callously, and there were numerous shootings at places, the biggest and the most tragic being in the Jallianwala Bagh at a non-violent and unarmed assembly of people.

REFERENCES

1. See M.A. Jinnah's speech in Legislative Assembly on the Rowlatt Bill, 7 February, 1919.
2. *Montagu Papers:* M.A. Jinnah to Chelmsford, dated 28 March, 1919.
3. P.E. Richards, *Indian Dust,* London, 1932, pp. 79-82.
4. *The Bombay Chronicle,* 25 January, 1919.
5. *The Hindu,* 22 January, 1919.
6. *Amrita Bazar Patrika,* 13 January, 1919.
7. *Punjabee,* 21 January, 1919.
8. *New India,* 11 January, 1919.
9. *D.P. Mishra, The History of Freedom Movement in Madhya Pradesh, Nagpur, 1956, pp. 278-79.*
10. *The Collected Works of Mahatma Gandhi,* Vol. XV, August 1918 — July 1919, p. 86.
11. *The Collected Works of Mahatma Gandhi, op. cit.,* p. 87.
12. J.B. Kripalani, *Gandhi'. His Life and Thought,* Delhi, 1970, p. 18.
13. *Ibid.,* p. 82.
14. Jawaharlal Nehru, *An Autobiography,* Delhi, 1962, p. 41.
15. The pledge was drafted on 24 February, 1919 and signed by those present at a meeting held at the Sabarmati Ashram.
16. *New India,* 3 March, 1919.
17. Home Pol. A, March 1919, F. 250.
18. *Young India,* 12 March, 1919.
19. *Ibid.*
20. *Ibid.*
21. *Ibid.*
22. *Ibid.*
23. *Ibid.*
24. *Ibid.*
25. Jawaharlal Nehru, *op. cit.,* p. 41.
26. Home Pol. A, March 1919, File 250.
27. *Ibid.,* August 1919, File 452-53.
28. Publications Division, Government of India, *Jallianwala Bagh,* Delhi, 1969, p. 2.
29. *The Bombay Chronicle*, 9 April, 1919.

30. *Ibid.*, 8 April, 1919.
31. *Ibid.*
32. *Ibid.*
33. *Ibid.*
34. *Ibid.*
35. *Ibid.*
36. *Ibid.*
37. *Ibid.*
38. *Ibid.*

Chapter 3
British Policy

In the Punjab, Amritsar was second in importance to Lahore, though in some respects it was more important even than Lahore. Its population in 1919 was 1,60,000. It is the city of the Golden Temple, the greatest place of worship for the Sikhs. Being the prominent commercial centre in the Punjab, it attracted travellers and visitors from all parts of the province and even from outside. Besides, it was one of the important centres of the Congress organisation in the province. It had also greatly developed socially, culturally, educationally and commercially. Flanked by a *mofussil* known for sturdy, prosperous and patriotic Hindus and Sikhs, any kind of sacrifice could be expected of them to save the honour of their motherland.

The Jallianwala Bagh, where the ghastly tragedy took place on 13 April, 1919, is situated almost in the heart of the city. The word *Bagh* is a misnomer. 'Jalle' is the caste name of original owner, 'wala' is the genitive termination; and the Bagh means a garden, is, in fact, an open piece of waste land surrounded by houses. It was, at that time, a private property, owned in common by several people. It was an irregular quadrangle, indifferently walled, and in most cases, the back walls of the houses surrounding it enclosed the quadrangle.

The Punjab Government reported about political condition in Amritsar thus: 'Orders having been received for the arrest and deportation of Dr. Kitchlew and Satyapal, the Deputy Commissioner sent for them on the morning of April 10th to his house from where they left in motors for Dharmsala at about 10.30 A.M. with an escort, in charge of Mr. Rehill,

Superintendent of Police. By about 11 A.M. the news of the arrests became known in the city, and ardent followers of the deportees went round urging the people to close their shops and assemble in the Aitchison Park, with the intention of proceeding to the Deputy Commissioner's House and demanding their release.

As it was expected that the arrests of Dr. Kitchlew and Satypal would cause a certain amount of excitement, it had been previously arranged that the Officer Commanding the Station would have a force of British infantry and some mounted men from the ammunition column in the Rambagh with which he was to hold the railway foot-bridge, the railway over-bridge and the hospital level-crossing while the Police Lines level crossing was to be held by the police. There was also an armed police reserve of 75 men at the City Kotwali.

Another mob of some thousands made a determined attempt to wreak its vengeance on British Banks and Christian religious buildings inside the city and to murder every Britisher they came across.

The National Bank of India was attacked and its Manager, Mr. Stewart was brutally murdered in one room and his assistant, Mr. Scott, was done to death in an adjoining one. The office furniture was heaped on the bodies and set on fire. The bank building was set fire too, and the store godowns were burnt open and their contents (piece-goods) looted.

The Chartered Bank was then attacked and the furniture and fittings smashed up, but every effort to break open the safe failed. The Manager, Mr. J.W. Thomson, and his assistant, Mr. Rose, were hiding at the top of a more than 50 yards away the mob bolting on their approach.

The Alliance Bank was similarly attacked; the mob breaking open the door, rushed upstairs into the office rooms. Mr. G.M. Thomson, the Manager, fired through a crevice in the door and killed one of the rioters. He then ran up the steps, to the top of the roof where he was followed by the mob who went up by another staircase in the piece-goods market. Driven from the roof, he came down the steps leading to his office, where he was seized, beaten and left for dead. Hearing that he was still alive, the mob rushed up again and finished him off and threw his body into the street below, where they heaped office furniture on it and set fire to it. The Bank safe was burst open and the contents, notes and cash were looted.

The Religious Society's Book Depot and Hall were burnt and the Indian Pastor, the Rev. Jaswant Singh and his wife who were living in the upper storey just managed to escape in time. The Town Hall and the Sub-Post Office attached to it were set on fire and completely gutted, while the Sub-Post Office at the Golden Temple, Majith Mandi and Dhab Basti Ram were looted.'

Besides Miss Sherwood, a mission lady, was caught in the heart of the city while on her way to a girls school and was beaten with shoes and sticks till she fell down exhausted when she was rescued by some Hindus living in the same quarter and carried to their house.[2] Outside the city, the mob set fire to Indian Christian Church, the bare walls of which only remained standing. The Normal Girls' School was attacked and clothes and books, etc., set on fire inside the building.[3]

A day prior to the tragedy at Jallianwala Bagh, a meeting attended by about 100 persons, was arranged in the campus of the Hindu Sabha School at Amritsar with the initiative of Hans Raj.[4] The idea was to have discussion about the arrests of Dr. Satyapal, Dr. Kitchlew and other local leaders and also to devise ways and means for the line of action to be taken in the near future.[5] The discussion led to a decision which was announced by Hans Raj that a meeting was to be held the next day in the campus of the Jallianwala Bagh under the presidentship of Lala Kanhaiya Lai, an esteemed resident of the town. It was also made clear that a statement from Dr. Kitchlew would be read by his wife before the assembly of the people there.[6] This decision was given a wide publicity in the whole city the next day before noon. Kanhaiya Lai denied before the committee his having been approached by anybody for presiding over the meeting of 13 April. It seems that his name was simply advertised to attract the audience to gather in a large number in the *Bagh*.

Soon after his arrival at Amritsar, Dyer halted at the railway station where he called a meeting of the local officials including the District Magistrate and the Superintendent of Police. He was apprised of the earlier events in the city, especially about Miss Sherwood who was shabbily treated by the local mob. Dyer felt much concerned about the loss of European lives, damage to government property and last but not the least about Miss Sherwood.

In order to have spacious place for himself and his force, Dyer, shifted his headquarters from railway station to Ram Bagh so that he could have a better glimpse of the civil population so far as their activities were concerned. Soon he had a round of the town to acquaint himself with the type of people and the prevailing political atmosphere. At places he was jeered at by the people and he made up his mind to arrest the ringleaders and punish them severely. Several of them were arrested, chained and put under army custody.

Besides Dyer was prompt enough to warn the inhabitants of Amritsar that if they made any kind of mischief tantamount to the breach of law and caused damage to the Government property, the offenders would be severely punished in accordance with the military law. Besides, they were warned not to hold any public meeting.

During these days, Amritsar presented a picture of an army camp. Lala Girdhari Lai, Deputy Chairman of the Punjab Chamber of Commerce, witnessed a grim picture on 11th April. He saw batches of policemen guarding the Amritsar railway station and the railway lines. The railway station itself looked like a military post. There was no proter nor conveyance of any kind. 'With great difficulty he reached the foot-bridge where there was a guard of some European soldiers who would not let any one enter the city without a thorough search. At every step outside the city one could see nothing but military or police at short distances with rifles and bayonets. Water supply had been stopped and so was the electric connection. All was dark in Amritsar on the eve of April 13, 1919.'

It was Sunday and the day of Baisakhi. In the Punjab, the harvest festival of Baisakhi is celebrated with great enthusiasm as the day which marks the end of the period of long and arduous labour. Peasants from all parts of the State assemble in towns and cities. For the Sikhs it is the day on which the Khalsa came into being. Naturally, the sacred city of the Golden Temple was filled on that day by people from all over the district many of whom had come to take a dip in the holy tank.

The public meeting at Jallianwala Bagh had been hastily arranged. In many ways, it was an expression of the spontaneous urge of the people of the sacred city to proclaim that their sensibilities had not been dulled by O' Dwyerean tyranny. After the events of April 10, 11 and 12, the people of Amritsar sought a way of expressing their many emotions—anger, grief and resolution. The announcements made in the different parts of the city about the meeting to be held were sketchy. Very few people knew who was organising the meeting and who would speak to them but they did not care. Their one intent was to assemble together and to say that the struggle was not over.[8]

On 13 April, General Dyer marched through the city with the civil officials and by the beating of a drum got the following official order announced at many places. 'It is hereby proclaimed to all whom it may concern that no person residing in the city is permitted or allowed to leave the city in his own private or hired conveyance or on foot without a pass from one of the following officers . . . No person residing in Amritsar city is permitted to leave his house after 8.00 P.M. Any person found in the streets after 8.00 P.M. is liable to be shot. No procession of any kind is permitted to parade the streets in the city or any part of the city or outside of it at any time. Any such processions or any gathering of four men will be looked upon and treated as an unlawful assembly and dispersed by forced of arms if necessary.

Soon after this proclamation, two persons were deputed to go round the city to announce a counter-proclamation, moderately, with the bang of tin, telling the people of Amritsar about a mass meeting to be arranged in the precincts of the Jallianwala Bagh on 13 April at 4.30 P.M. under the presidentship of Kanhaiya Lal, an eminent advocate of the town.

At about 12.45 P.M. General Dyer received the news that a huge meeting was to be held at Jallianwala Bagh at 4.30 P.M. on the same day. He admitted that he took no steps to prevent the meeting. 'I want you to explain', asked Lord Hunter, 'why you did not take measures to prevent the crowd from assembling at the Jallianwala Bagh?' The General answered, 'I went there as soon as I could. I had to organise my forces, to think the matter out ... I thought I had done enough in warning them not to meet.' Lord Hunter further asked, 'Did the making of dispositions necessitate the occupation of the time between 12.40 P.M. to 4 P.M. General Dyer answered, 'I did not believe that they would really meet, after all that I had done in the morning.'

According to the available evidence, prior to General Dyer's arrival the audience estimated at 20,000. Hans Raj and a few others were standing on an improvised platform. An aeroplane was hovering over the meeting before the arrival of the troops. Hans Raj announced in the audience not to be afraid. The audience included many boys and children, and some men had come with infants in their arms. The people assembled there had no *lathis* or any kind of weapon with them. Besides there were some C.I.D. men also at the meeting.

A few minutes before the sunset, Dyer with the company of young officers, Briggs and Anderson, fifty riflemen, forty Gurkhas aimed with their traditional weapons, the *kukris* and two armed cards, marched towards the Jallianwala Bagh with the clear intention of teaching the severest lesson of life to the peaceful assembly of the people. Undoubtedly the entrance of the *Bagh* was too narrow and, therefore, the armoured cars were parked out of the lane.

The organisers of this meeting showed much concern about the earlier happenings in the city when a few persons were killed as a result of promulgation of the Rowlatt Act which had afforded unchallenged powers to the bureaucracy. The main resolutions passed, therefore, dealt with these important issues—the first dealing with the severity of the application of the Rowlatt Bills and the second in connection with the firings of the previous day.

Dyer had a minute glimpse of the assembly of the people in the *Bagh* where the seventh speaker, Durga Das was speaking from the platform. The earlier six speakers were Rai Ram Singh, Dar Singh, Abdul Majid, Brij Gopi Nath, Hans Raj and Gurbaksh Rai. Dyer who was in independent command of the force under him was not to consult anybody at this point of time. He had already made up his mind to act in a way which might be a lesson-giving to the people of the Punjab. Not losing even a minute, he at once ordered his sepoys to adopt kneeling position, a usual posture for a soldier to fire. The firing order was given and the numerous volley of shots began to pierce into the bodies of the people in the *Bagh*.[9] It continued for about ten minutes till the ammunition was exhausted. It panicked the crowd and they ran pell-mell in all directions. Even the assurance from Durga Das that the firing consisted of blank shots, did not satisfy anybody.[10] In a moment, men were falling dead and wounded on the ground. Swinson stated thus:[11]

Immediately, the crowd panicked; rose to its feet and began streaming towards the narrow exits on the far side of the Bagh. Holding his position, Durga Das shouted that there was no need to worry; the troops were firing blanks. But even as he spoke, men began falling, the blood splurging red on their white *dhotis* and *patluns*. Das looked towards the troops in horror then dived behind the cover of the platform. The firing went on, the troops reloading in their own time.

Towards the exits on either flank, the crowds converged in their frantic effort to get away, jostling, clambering, elbowing and trampling over each other. Seeing this movement, Briggs drew Dyer's attention to it, and Dyer, mistakenly imagining that these sections of the crowd were getting ready to rush him, directed the fire of the troops straight at them. The result was horror, men screamed and went down to be trampled by those coming after. Some were hit again. In places the dead and wounded lay in heaps; men would go down wounded to find themselves immediately buried beneath a dozen others.

The firing still went on. Hundreds, abandoning all hope of getting away through the exits, tried the walls which in places were five feet high and at others seven or ten. . .

'Twenty thousand people were caught beneath the hall of bullets all of them frantically trying to escape from the quiet meeting-place which had suddenly become a screaming hell."[12]

When the firing ceased, nothing except dead bodies was visible in each and every corner of the *Bagh*. Some dead bodies were lying outside the *Bagh*. It so happened that the wounded persons who tried to run, could not survive and fell dead after a vain attempt to save themselves. The wounded were crying for help but nobody around the locality of the *Bagh* dared peep out of their houses for fear of being shot dead. The *Bagh* thus looked like a mini battlefield which was full of numerous corpses and wounded persons.

There had been no agreement on the exact figures of those killed in this ghastly tragedy. Dyer estimated between 200 and 300[13] and official figures were 379 killed and over 1200 wounded. Swami Shraddhanand gave the figures as 1500 killed, but Madan Mohan Malaviya stated that 1000 were killed. It is, however, probable that when 1,650 rounds were fired, the loss of lives must have been to the tune of a few hundreds and a much more number must have been wounded. A huge number of deaths were caused by the stampede that followed soon after the firing. The injured and the wounded might have concealed their identity for fear of the severe action under the martial law that was promulgated a few days after this tragedy. Hence their number could not be properly ascertained.

This type of ghastly and gruesome tragedy perpetrated on a few hundred persons was indeed an unprecedented phenomenon in the history of India. This was done by a senior army official who gave no serious thought to his inhuman action which he undertook to satisfy his personal whims and fancies. There had been firings on meetings, processions and mobs earlier by the British bureaucracy in India, but this kind of tragic drama as was enacted on a peaceful assembly in Jallianwala Bagh was never heard of. The justification for firing put forward by General Dyer does not satisfy an impartial observer of the events at Amritsar.

Dyer gives an unconvincing reason to the fact that the mob which was considerable in number on account of the celebration of the Baisakhi day would have become unmanageable and would have overpowered him and his small force rendering him to be too late to control the critical situation in the city. This was simply a working of his mind which was not based on any kind of logic. About twenty thousand persons had gathered in the Jallianwala Bagh to hear the earlier story of the arrest and deportation of their two prominent leaders, Dr. Saifuddin Kitchlew and Dr. Satyapal and the misrule which was tantamount to various kinds of repressions and administrative lapses on the part of Michael O'Dwyer. They would have dispersed peaceful in various parts of the city as well as to their respective villages from where they had come to Amritsar with the twin purpose of paying visit to the golden temple as well as showing their sense of unity, solidarity and patriotism to a common cause.

It is unfortunate to hear Dyer saying that the assembly of people in the Jallianwala Bagh consisted of defiant characters and of criminal revolutionaries who were bent upon doing damage to human life and property. This kind of opinion smacks of unwarranted prejudice of highest degree. From alt evidence available to us it was a non-violent assembly of peace- loving citizens of Amritsar and innocent people from the *mofussil*. To expect any kind of violent behaviour from them after the dispersal of such a meeting was only a mistaken notion in Dyer's mind. Already much had happened in various parts[1] of the city and the local citizens had been adequately punished for that.

It was heinous crime, nay immoral as well as illegal, to shoot such a big number of people to death like sheep and goats in shambles. A mob of this magnitude or even of more or lesser magnitude could be dispersed in a way with a loss of very few lives or no loss of life at all. No law of the land permits any official—military or civil—to shoot people to death without a clear-cut warning for dispersal announced on the mike. In the normal procedure, when the mob is unruly, violent and uncontrollable, firing is done in the air or in a way, where people are injured on legs, etc., but not get killed. In this case, it appears that Dyer gave no warning to the people assembled in the *Bagh* and resorted to unprecedented firing thus violating the implications of the existing law. Granted that under the martial law regime, an army commander wields a kind of superpowers in his hands, but this should never be tantamount to taking lives of people in a way it was done in Jallianwala Bagh. Dyer tried to give statements before the Hunter Committee which were evasive and unconvincing. He replied, 'I could have dispersed them for some time. Then they would all come back and laughed at me and I considered I would be making myself a fool.' When this kind of thinking lurks in the minds of a martial law administrator, it is indeed difficult to expect justice and fair play from him in this kind of situation.

The amount of ammunition used and the duration of firing are highly questionable. Dyer used about 1600 rounds and the firing continued for about ten minutes. The firing was done at low height so that it could be more effective, and its worst feature was that it stopped when the ammunition was exhausted. It is indeed unfortunate that no local civil official was consulted and takes into confidence in this kind of severe action by Dyer. A civil official is fully conversant with the political and other views of the people whom he administers. Miles Irving, the Deputy Commissioner of Amritsar, was not consulted before the firing in the *Bagh*.

When the firing was over, Dyer and his men left the precincts of the Jallianwala Bagh which was full of dead bodies. Numerous persons were badly wounded and they were crying for help. No medical aid was available for them. They also breathed their last in the next few hours. Many lives could have been saved with the timely provision of medical aid.

The government of India passed the following order on 13th April, 1919:[14] 'Whereas the Governor-General-in-Council is satisfied that a state of open rebellion against the authority of the Government exists in the districts of Lahore and Amritsar in the Province of the Punjab.

'Now, therefore, in exercise of the powers conferred by section 2 of the Bengal State Offences Regulation, 1804, the Governor-General-in-Council is hereby pleased to suspend the functions of the ordinary Criminal Courts within those Districts in so far as the trial of persons of the classes referred to in the said Regulation taken in arms in open hostility to the British Government or in the act of opposing by force of arms the authority of the same, or in the actual commission of any overt act of rebellion against the State or in the act of openly siding and abetting the enemies of the British government within the said Districts, is concerned, and to establish Martial Law within the said Districts.

'The Governor-General-in-Council is also pleased to direct the immediate trial by courts-martial of all persons owing allegiance to the British Government, either in consequence of their having been born, or of their residents within its territories and under its protection, who shall be taken in arms in open hostility to the British Government, or in the act of opposing by force of arms the authority of the same or in the actual commission of any overt act of rebellion against the State, or in the act of openly aiding and abetting the enemies of the British government within any part of the said Districts.'[15] Similar orders were issued by the government of India in connection with Gujranwala, Lyallpur and other areas in the Punjab.

Girdhari Lai, a prominent local Congressman, happened to watch the scene from a house overlooking the *Bagh*. He saw hundreds of persons killed on the spot. The worst part of the whole thing was that firing was directed towards the gates through which the people were turning out. There were small outlets, four or five in all, and bullets actually rained over the people at all these gates. Many persons got trampled under the feet of the rushing crowds and thus lost their lives. Besides, blood was pouring in profusion. Even those who lay flat on the ground were shot. There were heaps of dead bodies scattered at different directions. The dead bodies were of grown-up people and young boys also. Some of them had their heads cut open, others had eyes shot, and nose, chest, arms or legs shattered. 'I think there must have been over 1,000 dead bodies in the garden then. ... I saw people were burying up and many had to leave them dead and wounded, because they were afraid of being fired upon again after 8 P.M.'

Ratan Devi told the Congress Enquiry Committee: 'I was in my house near Jallianwala Bagh when I heard shots fired ... I got up at once as I was anxious because my husband had gone to the *Bagh* . . . There I saw heaps of bodies and I began to search for my husband . . . By this time it was 8 o'clock and no one could stir out of his house because of the curfew order. I stood on, waiting and crying. At about eight thirty a Sikh gentleman came ... I entreated the Sikh gentleman to help me in removing my husband's body to a dry place, for that place was overflowing with blood. He took the body by the head and I by the legs and we carried it to a dry place and laid it down on a wooden block. I waited up to 10.00 P.M. . . . Then I started towards Katra again and saw an old man. I repeated the whole of my sad story to him. He took pity on me and asked the men to go with me. But they said that it was 10.00 o'clock and that they would not like to be shot down. . . So I went back and seated myself by the side of dead husband. Accordingly, I found a bamboo stick which I kept in my hand to keep off dogs. I saw men writhing in agony . . . A boy of about twelve years old in agony entreated me not to leave the place ... I asked him if he wanted any wrap and if he was feeling cold I could spread it over him. He asked for water, but water could not be procured at that place. I was all alone the whole night in a solitary jungle. Nothing but the barking of dogs, the braying of donkeys and the groans of the wounded was audible.'

During his brief halt at Amritsar, Jawaharlal Nehru recorded a statement by Maqbul Mohammad, an advocate of High Court and a resident of Amritsar. 'On the 10th just after the firing stopped at the carriage overbridge I went to the hospital and brought Dr. Dhanpat Rai[17] there. Mr. G.S. Salaria,[18] Dr. Dhanpat Rai and I first came to dress a stout young lad of about 18 who lay badly wounded with his intestines and abdominal viscera turned out and lying in the dusty road. He made signs for water. I brought it in my cap and poured some water into his mouth. He revived a little and could then blust out a few words.

Dr. Dhanpat Rai then came to attend on him. The youngman with faltering accents said, '*meri koi ummeed naheeti, mere nal ke bhai ka iruizam karo.*' He stopped, then gasped brokenly: "Hindu-Musulman ki Jai" and expired.

Miles Irving explained thus:[19] 'Generally speaking I as Deputy Commissioner acted as intermediary between the people and the military . . . The order about crawling past the picket at the place where Miss Sherwood was announced by General Dyer to the troops at the same time as he wanted them against any private act of reprisals. It was also announced to the civilians in the Fort and he explained to me that his idea was to emphasise in the most public and striking way the enormity of an offence against a woman, and by so doing to take men's minds off the idea of private reprisals for an offence so calculated to provoke them.'

In Amritsar, Dyer now had the undisputed control. On the night of the 13th, when some shopkeepers came to him and begged permission to open their premises, he granted it, and business was in a normal state the next morning. The curfew was also relaxed, the water supply restored, and life returned almost to normal.

'On 19th April, martial law was formally proclaimed, and a great combing of the city began to find the criminals and agitators. The police, humiliated by the crowd on the 10th, began taking their revenge, and men brought in for questioning let alone the main suspects, had a rough time of it. A triangle was set up where twenty-five offenders were later flogged. It was at this time that Dyer committed the stupidest act of his entire career, when he instituted the 'Crawling Order' which laid down that Indians passing down the Kucha Kanarianwala, the lane where Miss Sherwood had been beaten, should between 6 A.M. and 8 P.M. be made to go down on all face and crawl.'[20]

The police began to arrest people indiscriminately. There was no break after that and persons in every sphere of life were arrested from day to day, while employed peacefully in their occupations. No charge was stated against them; they were handcuffed and put into the lock-up for days and months, without being informed what they were accused of and no opportunity was ever allowed to them to see or consult friends or relations.

'His (Dyer's) only concern seemed to be to add to his laurels of the Afghan war by another display of what he considered to be military efficiency. For him even an unarmed crowd was a hostile army. "For me", he said, "the battlefield of France and Amritsar was the same." Before leaving Jullundur for Amritsar he told his son that a big show was coming.'

A proclamation was made in Amritsar and the surrounding villages inviting all persons who had any information regarding the names of those who had met with deaths. Instructions were issued to the local authorities there to encourage men to come forward and give information they possessed. 'Every possible step was taken in that direction. The result of the enquiry was that the total number of casualties amounted to 291, and any further number suggested by any body must be taken with great discretion.'[21]

On 14 April, a meeting of the local residents, Municipal Commissioners, Magistrates and merchants was called at the Kotwali, where Mr. Kitchin, the Commissioner made the following speech: 'Do you people want peace or war? We are prepared in every way. The Government is all powerful. *Sarkar* has conquered Germany and is capable of doing everything. The General will give orders today. The city is in his possession. I can do nothing. You will have to obey order.'

After this the Commissioner went away. General Dyer with Miles Irving, Rehill, Ploomer and a few military soldiers came about 5 P.M. the same day. He rushed into the room, followed by others, all exceedingly angry and delivered a speech in Urdu. The following is the translation:

'You people know well that I am a sepoy and soldier. Do you want war or peace? If you wish for war, the Government is prepared for it, and if you want peace, then obey my orders and open all your shops; else I will shoot. For me the battlefield of France or Amritsar is the same. I am a military man and I will go straight. Neither shall I move to the right not to the left. Speak up, if you want war. In case there is to be peace, my order is to open all shops at once. You people talk against the Government, and persons educated in Germany and Bengal talk sedition. 1 shall report all these. Obey orders. I do not wish to have anything else. I have served in the military for over 30 years. 1 understand the Indian sepoy and the Sikh people very well. You will have to observe peace, otherwise the shops will be opened by force and by rifles. You must inform me of the *budmashes*. I will shoot them. Obey orders and open shops. Speak up if you want war.'[22]

General Dyer's speech was followed by that of Miles Irving, the Deputy Commissioner of Amritsar. The two sentences of his speech may be quoted here. 'You have committed a bad act in killing the English. The revenge will be taken upon you and your children.'[23]

These speeches in the shape of severe warning from no less officials than Dyer and the Deputy Commissioner had salutary effect on the local commercial class which had witnessed a gruesome tragedy unprecedented in the history of India. Next day, all the shops were opened. A common person would have thought that with the retribution of the 13th April, the authoritative speeches of the 14th and the opening of the shops, the ordinary civil rule would be resumed, but it was not to be. The revenge had not yet been fully taken. To gear up the machinery of the Government in a way the British administrators wanted, martial law was proclaimed which remained in force up to the 9th June and the life of the local people was made difficult and intolerable in numerous ways.

The street in which Miss Sherwood was assaulted was set apart for flogging people and for making those who passed through it to crawl on their bellies. All were made to *salam*, in theory British officials only, but in practice every English man, on pain of being arrested and suffering indignities. Flogging was administered publicly and otherwise, even for trivialities. All the lawyers of the town were made special constables without cause and made to work like ordinary coolies. Indiscriminate arrests were affected of persons, irrespective of their social status and position, and during detention they were subjected to humiliations, discomforts and indescribable tortures for the purpose of extorting confession or evidence, or for the purpose of merely humiliating them. Besides, special tribunals were appointed for trying offences, which resulted in gross injustice in the name of law, leaving the aggrieved parties without a right to appeal.

The lane in which the crawling took place was a narrow and thickly populated place, with double-storey buildings on either side of it, and with numerous blind alloys shooting out the lane and containing several houses. For the inhabitants of the lane, if they wanted to make any purchases or to go to the city, there was no option but to pass through some part of it, and, therefore, to crawl in and out. Besides sanitary or medical service could only be rendered on condition of crawling. The full length of the lane was about 150 yards. In the middle of it was seen an oblong marked 'Tiktiki' which was the specially erected flogging booth. The order remained in force for eight days. Although General Dyer had called it 'going on all fours' and it had been called 'hand and knee order' by the press, the process consisted of persons lying flat on their bellies and crawling exactly like the reptiles. Any lifting of the knees or bending thereof brought the rifle butts on the backs of the persons who were made to crawl. The whole movement had therefore, to be performed by movement of the belly and the arms. The lane, like most Indian lanes, was dirty and full of the usual rubbish, not excluding grit.

The promulgation of martial law in various districts of the Punjab was a phenomenon autocratic in nature which was disliked and criticised by the national leadership. The justification of its promulgation on the part of the government was founded on an old regulation of the *Raj*. By article 2 of the Bengal Regulation Act 10 of 1804 the Governor-in-Council was entitled in direct any public authority or officer to order the suspension, wholly or partially, of the functions of the ordinary criminal courts of judicature.

The Lieutenant-Governor of the Punjab with the concurrence of the General Officer Commanding the 16th Division and Chief Justice of the High Court made declaration of martial law at

Lahore and Amritsar on 15th April. Similar applications were made in respect of Gujranwala on 15th April, Gujarat on 18th April and Lyallpur on 20th April, Sanction having been given to the declaration of martial law as asked, proclamations to this effect were made in these districts on 16th, 19th and 24th April respectively. On the declaration of martial law in the districts of Lahore and Amritsar, General Beynon, commanding the 16th Division at Lahore, assumed command. Colonel Money was appointed under him to administer martial law. The officers commanding in Amritsar, in Lahore civil areas and in Lahore Cantonment administered martial law.

The powers of area officers as regards punishment were under the proclamations, limited to sentencing an offender to two years' rigorous imprisonment or fine not exceeding Rs. 1,000 or both, and to whipping in addition to or in lieu of any other punishment.[21]

In the first half of April, 1919, the government of the Punjab reported: 'The Satyagraha agitation and the Delhi riots have latterly monopolised attention. Violence and mis-representation had reached such a pitch that Government has been constrained to take stringent action . . . The extraordinary vigilance and intemperate attacks on Government which have characterised almost the whole Indian Press for some time past are, as is becoming increasingly apparent, largely responsible; for the present state of the country.'[23]

On 19 April 1919, General Beynon issued a martial law proclamation containing certain regulations that were to be enforced within the limits of the 16th Indian Division in all; places to which martial law had been or might be extended- This document defined as martial law offences the act of being in arms against the State or inciting others to be in arms; assisting or harbouring rebels; failure to report gatherings of rebels. Use of language or issuing proclamations likely to foment rebellion or promote hostility between different classes of His Majesty's subjects; interference with railways, canals or telegraphs; possession of a motor vehicle without permit; departure from or entry to a proclaimed area save under conditions to be prescribed; convening or attending a meeting of more than five persons; escaping or attempting to escape from legal custody; disobeying an order given by a civil military officer in the execution of his duty when administering martial law; disseminating false intelligence likely to cause alarm or despondency; destroying martial law notices; refusing to give a correct name and address on demand and committing an act in prejudice of good order of public safety or calculated to hamper or mislead His Majesty's forces.[26]

Offences against these regulations were to be tried summarily by officers known as area officers. In Amritsar district, the General Officer Commanding the Jullundur Brigade became the administrator of martial law, and had at first one area officer of Major's rank.[27] Lahore district was divided into two areas (*a*) the Lahore Civil Area; and (*b*) Lahore district, outside the city, the latter being in the hands of the General Officer Commanding Lahore Brigade. The civil area was under Lt. Colonel F. Johnson who was given three officers, of or above Major's rank, as area officers. The administrator in the Lahore district area was subsequently given a separate area officer of Captain's rank for Kasur.[28]

At the time of the proclamation of martial law at Gujranwala, the General Officer Commanding, 2nd Rawalpindi Division, issued a proclamation on 20 April almost in the same terms to that issued by General Beynon.[29] The administration of martial law was carried on by the General Officer Commanding, Sialkot Brigade who moved his headquarters to Wazirabad. Besides, the Deputy Commissioner of Gujranwala was notified as area officer for Gujranwala; an officer of Major's rank as area officer for Wazirabad, the Joint Deputy Commissioner for the Sheikhupura area and an officer of Captain's rank for Hafizabad. Gujrat and Lyallpur both came under the general Rawalpindi proclamation. Besides, on 24 May, 1919, orders were passed by the Punjab Government directing the precensorship of the same newspapers, viz., *Congress, Vijaya, Qaum* and *Inqilab*.[30]

At Lahore, the position was no better. Colonel Johnson, incharge of martial law administration, had constituted summary courts. He himself tried cases. Two hundred seventy-seven persons were thus tried of whom 201 were convicted. The maximum sentence was two years' imprisonment, thirty stripes and also a fine of one thousand rupees. The highest number of stripes was thirty, the lowest five. These men were publicly flogged until an order came to the effect that they were not to be so flogged. There was hardly any medical examination. When Lord Hunter asked him whether he never imagined the punishment had serious effect, he answered, 'I cannot imagine it.' In his opinion it was 'the kindliest method of punishment'. To Mr. Justice Rankin he said, he terrorised people, and dozens and dozens of sentences were saved. Justice Rankin thought that it was a little strong to suggest that whipping should be regarded as the most efficacious and convenient method of summarily dealing with masses of people in minor breaches and asked Col. Johnson whether it should not be rather exceptional and the answer was, 'I hardly agree with you. You have a very great population. You are creating new offences by the issue of these orders. If the jail is the only punishment, it would not affect this population here very much. The jail is an extraordinarily comfortable place from the general standard of household in the city. They are well-fed in the Central Jail and one would soon have got used to the conditions. We were going to have the whole lot of them. I feared the jail would be filled.'[31]

Colonel Johnson had commandeered 800 *tongas* which number was finally reduced to 200, and these were detained up to the time the martial law was in force. He also commandeered all the motor cars belonging to Indians. He restricted travelling by railways, so as "to limit the activities of gentlemen who might proceed outside the city to the district with a view to cause trouble there. He issued an order stopping all the free restaurants. He regulated the prices of food stuffs. He dispossessed licence-holders of their guns and his order had to be restrained by the government in regard to those who were known to be men of 'undoubted loyalty'. He confirmed the orders that were issued by the Deputy Commissioner closing the Badshahi Mosque, and it was permitted to be opened only on an undertaking being given by the trustees that 'No Hindu would be allowed to enter the Badshahi Mosque'.[32]

Colonel Johnson's railway travelling order, besides being general, was particularly aimed at lawyers' clerks and their messengers. It is well-known how far this bias against the lawyer class was carried, how lawyers from outside the Punjab were refused admittance on the ground that they might also disseminate sedition. 'Even a scholarly lawyer of Mr. Manohar Lai's standing, respectability, known loyalty. . . could not count upon being safe from the attentions of the Martial Law Officers.[33] He was arrested on 18th April, 1919 as a trustee of *The Tribune* newspaper published from Lahore.[34] There was no warrant nor was he apprised of any kind of charge under which he had been arrested. He stated the pathetic circumstances under which he was arrested and subjected to serious mental depression and torture. 'On my arrest at my house, I had barely two minutes to take leave of my wife and children, and I was given no indication of where I was to be taken. . . I was removed by the Police from the Telegraph Office to the Central Jail, Lahore, where after the usual ceremonies at the gate, of depositing watch and chain, pencil, loose cash, etc., and signing the Register by my thumb impression only, I was taken into a cell in the Ward No. 14 of the jail. This ward is meant for condemned prisoners, or those awaiting for capital or similar offences. In this cell, I was supplied after a time with two filthy jail blankets, and two iron basins to eat and drink out of it. After about three hours, I was transferred to another part of the jail, known as the *Chakkis, i.e.*, a series of cells furnished with arrangements for grinding corn. . . All our sanitary and other arrangements were inside the small cells, consisting of stinking earthen vessels, cleansed twice a day.

'My wife and children had no idea of where I was confined till late in the afternoon of the day of my arrest. I was allowed no communication with them, except for the postcard I was able to send through the Superintendent of the Jail, on Saturday afternoon.

'On Wednesday, the 23rd I was transferred to the European ward, where I was comparatively more comfortable, having considerable liberty of movement, and because of the accommodation, and clean lavatory and washing arrangements and a small library.'[35]

The following are the figures of the sentences of whipping inflicted in the five districts under martial law, ranging from 3 to 80. Lahore 80; Kasur 79; Chuharkana 40; Gujranwala 24; Amritsar 32; Gujrat 3 and Lyallpur nil. This makes the total of 258.[36] The Secretary of State showed concern over the manner of flogging and whipping people in public in his communication to Viceroy[37] on 28 April, 1919, 'If we are challenged it may be difficult to convince public of appropriateness of action in these cases and I shall be glad of your views.'

Thus the regime of General Dyer perpetrated numerous kinds of other punishments which were degradation personified. The water supply and the electric supply to the people of Amritsar were stopped thus putting them to unthinkable harassment. The prohibition of the issue of third-class tickets to the railway passengers involved a general apprehension by many Indian people. More than two persons were prohibited from any kind of meeting. Vehicles were commandeered and prices of commodities were fixed by military authorities. The censoring of the press was so strict that the ingress and egress of people to and from the Punjab was rigidly regulated.

The suffering of the student community at Lahore was unprecedented during the period of martial law. They suffered an unbearable indignities, indescribable harassment and indiscriminate floggings at the hands of the authorities. The punishments were tantamount to expulsions, rustications, detention, forfeiture of scholarships, forfeiture of fee concessions and refusal of re-admissions.

REFERENCES

1. Home Pol. Deposit, June 1919, File 23.
2. *Ibid.*
3. *Ibid.*
4. See Disorders Inquiry Committee, Vol. Ill, pp. 82, 112.
5. *Ibid.*
6. *Ibid.*
7. Quoted in Report of Indian National Congress, *op. cit.,* p. 44.

8. *Ibid.*
9. Arthur Swinson, *Six Minutes to Sunset,* London, 1964, pp. 47-8.
10. *Ibid.*
11. *Ibid.*
12. *Ibid.*
13. Home Pol. A., February 1920, File 347-58.
14. *Ibid.,* May 1919, File 74-108.
15. *Ibid.*
16. *Ibid.*
17. A medical practitioner and a Congressman of Amritsar.
18. A leading barrister of Amritsar arrested for participation in the *Satyagraha Day* meeting held on 6 April, 1919.
19. Home Pol. Deposit, October 1919, File 62.
20. Arthur Swinson, *op. cit.,* p. 63.
21. Home Pol. Deposit, October, 1919, File 31.
22. Quoted in the Congress Report, *op. cit.,* p. 59.
23. *Ibid.*
24. Area Officers sitting as Summary Courts dealt with cases against 543 persons of whom 386 were convicted.
25. Home Pol. Deposit, July 1919, File 46.
26. *Report of Disorders Enquiry Committee, 1919-1920, Calcutta, 1920, p. 125.*
27. *Ibid.*
28. *Ibid.*
29. Home Pol. Deposit, June 1919, File 26.
30. *Ibid.*
31. Disorders Inquiry Report, p, 82.
32. See the Congress Report, *op. cit.,* p. 81.
33. He was an M.A. Bar-at-Law; advocate High Court, Punjab; Fellow and a Member of the Syndicate, Punjab University and the President, Forman Christian College Graduates' Union.
34. At present, *The Tribune* is published from Chandigarh.
35. The Congress Report, *op. cit.,* pp. 82-83.
36. It does not include any flogging resorted to when the mobile columns visited the various villages.
37. Home Pol. Deposit, May 1919, File 4.

Chapter 4
Bureaucratic Reaction

On 14 October, 1919, the Governor-General-in Council with the approval of the Secretary of State for India, decided to appoint a committee to investigate the disturbances in Punjab, Delhi and Bombay and pinpoint their causes and the measures taken to cope with them. The President of the Disorders Inquiry Committee was Lord William Hunter, ex-Solicitor-General and the Senator of the College of Justice in Scotland, and the other members were G.C. Rankin, Judge of the High Court, Calcutta; W.F. Rice, Additional Secretary to the Government of India, Home Department; Major General George Barrow, Commanding the Peshawar Division; Pandit Jagat Narayan, Thomas Smith, both members of the Legislative Council, United Provinces; Chimanlal Harilal Setalvad, Advocate, High Court, Bombay; and Sardar Sahibzada Sultan Ahmed Khan, Muntazim-ud-Doula, Member for Appeals, Gwalior State. The secretary of the committee was H.G. Stokes,[1] Secretary to the Government of Madras. The committee which was to conduct its inquiries in public as well as *in camera,* was required to submit its report to the government of India.[3]

In their final findings, the members of the committee were not unanimous in their opinion: obviously the report although published in one volume, had two phases—the first dealing with the majority report agreed upon by William Hunter, G.C. Rankin, W.F. Rice, George Barrow and Thomas Smith, and the second dealing with the minority report signed by Jagat Narayan, C.H. Setalvad and Sultan Ahmed.[3]

The majority report dealt with the occurrences in Delhi, Bombay Presidency, Punjab, declaration of martial law and the kind of administration in these provinces. The first outbreak occurred in Delhi on 30 March, 1919 when a general *hartal* was declared as part of Gandhi's call for *satyagraha* against the Rowlatt legislation. It took place with success in the sense that shops both of Hindus and Muslims were closed and business was brought to a standstill in the city. The people of the city observed the day as one of fasting and abstinence from work. A considerable number of them went to Delhi Railway Station, where they endeavoured to get the vendors of refreshments at the third class refreshment room to abstain from work and join with them in their *hartal*. On refusal of vendors, they dragged the contractor who was hurt in the scuffle. On this when the railway police arrested two persons, the mob got infuriated and began to demonstrate, obstructing and finally stopping traffic at the railway station. The civil authorities requisitioned the services of the army and this force proved effective and the crowd of people was pressed back across Queen's Road by the soldiers. Bricks were thrown at policemen and the soldiers and the situation became serious when the crowd was completely out of control. At this, the mob was fired at as a result of which two or three persons were killed and several wounded.[1] After the firing, the crowd moved towards the Town Hall and Chandni Chowk. The police were pelted with missiles by the crowd which refused to disperse although requested to do so by some of the police constables in front. At this firing was again resorted to and as a result thereof eight persons were killed and about a dozens were wounded.[5]

On 1st April, shops were opened in the city and a meeting was held at the Fatehpuri mosque where Hindus also participated in large numbers. On 9th April, Gandhi who was on his way from Bombay to Delhi, was stopped at a small station, Palwal, in the Punjab. He was taken under police custody, and this news spread throughout the city like wildfire. Next day there was a general *hartal* in the city as the word came in the evening of that day of the serious occurrences at Amritsar and Lahore. Although there was a collection of crowds of people in some places, there was no unpleasant incident in the city. The *hartal*, however, continued in spite of the efforts of the officials who had arranged numerous meetings with the local leaders. No disturbance occurred in Delhi after 17th April. On 18th April most of the shops in the suburbs of the city and a certain number in the main bazar opened, while on the 19th shops in the Chandni Chowk opened and the *hartal* was brought to an end.[6] The committee observed thus: 'The outbreak in Delhi on 30th March arose out of the *hartal* held in connection with Mr. Gandhi's passive resistance movement started as a protest against the Rowlatt legislation . . . Mr. Gandhi resolved to have a *hartal* held throughout India on a particular day as an indication of national disapproval of the Government's policy and there was considerable agitation connected therewith. There is no doubt that the feeling against the Rowlatt Act was very widespread. Bitter speeches were made against it when it was before the Legislative Council. Wild rumours were circulated as to its effect. As examples of these rumours we were told that it was said that, under the Act, the police would have power to arrest any three or four men conversing together, that nobody would be allowed to own more than a certain amount of land, and that nobody would be allowed to marry without leave from Government. These and similar rumours were widely circulated and believed by the illiterate population who were not familiar with the provisions of the Act. So far as Delhi is concerned, it is not said that the political leaders were responsible for the circulation of these rumours. The worst thing alleged against them is, that they did not deny the truth of the rumours and did not trouble themselves to explain the nature and effect of the provisions of the Act which they were denouncing.'

As regards the measures taken by the authorities to deal with the disturbances, the committee stated that these were adequate and reasonable. Martial law was not proclaimed though the situation was so serious that the Chief Commissioner applied to the Government of India for authority to declare martial law. Throughout the critical period he received assistance from the military in quelling disturbances, patrolling of the streets and maintenance of law and order. On all the occasions firing was ordered after the patience of those entrusted with the duty of maintaining public peace and order had been sorely tried and all reasonable efforts had been made to induce the crowd to disperse peacefully. In no case was firing continued longer than was necessary to achieve the 'legitimate object of restoring order and preventing a disastrous outbreak of violence.[7]

The committee gave its findings about the occurrence of disturbances in Ahmedabad, Viramgam, Nadiad, Kaira and Bombay. Ahmedabad with a population of four lakhs, seventy-eight mills and forty thousand workmen was the centre of numerous political meetings at which the doctrine of Home Rule was advocated by prominent leaders. Many branches of the Home Rule League were established in Ahmedabad and the neighbouring district. A special feature of the situation was the particular interest taken by the people in Mahatma Gandhi and his *satyagraha* movement.

On 23rd February. 1919, a meeting of the Ahmedabad branch of the Home Rule League was held to protest against the Rowlatt Bills. From this meeting, the origin of *satyagraha* movement could be traced. On the following day another meeting was held in Gandhi's *ashram*. It was attended by representative Home Rulers from Bombay who decided to start a passive resistance campaign against the proposed Rowlatt legislation. A manifesto was drawn up and approved containing a form of oath to be taken by the members of the *satyagraha sabha* to refuse to obey the Rowlatt Bills, if passed and such other laws as a committee, to be appointed later, were to decide.

The agitation against the Rowlatt agitation was vigorously maintained all through the month of March, particularly in Ahmedabad and Kaira districts. Feelings of irritation and anger against the government were roused among the masses. The news of Gandhi's arrest spread rapidly and caused great excitement. The mill-hands ceased work, and the shops in the city were closed. The secretary of the *satyagraha* sabha issued a circular for the Congress workers in which he declared about Gandhi's arrest. At this, they felt much excited. The streets were filled with disorderly crowds who enforced *hartal* and compelled persons in conveyances to get down and walk as a sign of mourning.[8]

The 11th April was marked by disturbances of great violence, requiring an extensive use of military force. The mob burnt the *Mamlatdar's*[9] court-house, the telegraph office, the post office at Delhi Gate and two police chowkies. Another mob went to the electric power station, assaulted a British official there and stopped the working of the power station. Thus the riotous crowds were everywhere in the city, breaking street-lamps and doing other damage. Some police constables were caught and stripped of their uniforms and driven away. Even in the presence of troops the mobs showed little restraint and on several occasions the parties of troops, sent to assist the civil authority in the maintenance of order, had to resort to firing. The total number of casualties caused by the firing was about six or seven. 'When night fell, the city and suburbs except on the north-west were still in the hands of the rioters who during the night burnt some minor government and municipal buildings in the mill area and suburbs, had taken refuge in the Shahibagh or at the railway station, where they were under military protection.'

The military force remained on vigil in many areas of the city. The electric power station being closed, the city and railway station were without light. The drainage pumping engine had ceased to work and the municipal conservancy staff had virtually disappeared. The committee reported that 'The need of effective action speedily to restore order was imperative.' The Government ordered that 'Any gathering of over ten individuals collected in one spot will be fired at. Any single individual seen outside any house who does stop and come up when challenged between the hours of 7 P.M. and 6 A.M. will be shot.'

Meanwhile Gandhi and Miss Ansuya Sarabhai arrived at Ahmedabad on 13th April. The former at once visited the Commissioner and arrangements were made that the proclamation issued by the military authorities should be withdrawn on the 14th April. On that day, Gandhi addressed a huge meeting of people in which he upbraided them for their violence and exhorted them to resume their lawful occupations. The committee noted in its report, 'His address had a very beneficial effect and the disturbances at Ahmedabad practically came to an end on the 14th April.'[10]

The committee recorded that during the disturbances there were two fatal casualties on the side of law and order, namely, the armed constable who was thrown from the balcony and Sergeant Fraser. Among the rioters 28 were known to have been killed and 123 wounded ... It is probable that there were more, but the others have not been traced'. The number of rounds fired during the whole period was 139 by the police and 639 by the troops. Telegraph wires were cut at eight places in Ahmedabad and at fourteen places outside. The value of the property destroyed by the rioters at Ahmedabad was approximately nine and a half lakhs of rupees. The committee opined, 'We are of opinion that the measures taken by the authorities to deal with the disturbances were appropriate. The use of military force was unavoidable and the rioters alone were responsible for the casualties which ensued. The control of the city was in the hands of the military for less than two days and this has been referred to as a period of martial law. But beyond maintaining order and issuing the proclamation on 12th April, the military authorities did not interfere with matters of administration. The so-called martial law orders were drastic; but the situation was most serious. The belief that all groups of more than ten men would be fired on without warning did much to restore order, and it appears that this instruction was not in fact literally carried out.'

Besides there were disturbances at Viramgam where the people took their cue from Ahmedabad. On 11th April there was a general *hartal* in the town. Mill-hands struck work and all shops were closed. The next day, the mob broke out in violent disorder, murdered an Indian magistrate, set on fire the railway station, cut telegraph wires, put the police *chowki* on fire, and plundered and burned the local post office. The police resorted to firing which caused a complete dispersion of the rioters. A detachment of troops arrived from Ahmedabad and took charge of the town. This marked the end of the disturbances and no further outbreak occurred. The shops of Viramgam reopened on the 13th April. According to the report of the committee, six persons were killed and eighteen wounded. The value of the property destroyed by the rioters exceeded two lakhs of rupees. 'The unarmed police in the town were helpless and disappeared. The force used against the rioters . . . was certainly not excessive. If greater force could have been applied at an early stage, the commission of atrocious murder[11] and much destruction of property might have been prevented . . . Apart from the murder, fifty men were tried for offences connected with the occurrence, of whom twenty-seven were convicted and the rest acquitted.'

In Kaira, people observed *hartal* through the district and at Nadiad, the mill-hands struck work and all shops were closed. On the night of the 11th April, a party from Nadiad removed a rail from the permanent way at a place about one and half a mile south of the Nadiad railway station. The troops train arrived shortly afterwards, travelling at high speed. The train was derailed at the gap, but was brought to a stand without loss of life. The actual result was that the arrival of the troops at Ahmedabad was delayed for some hours. The next day, railway line was again damaged within a few miles of Nadiad; the telegraph wires were cut; rail-keys removed, telegraph posts pulled down, insulators smashed and the sleepers of a culvert set on fire. Besides at two other places in the neighbourhood, Vadod and Anand, telegraph wires were cut on the night of the 11th April. In view of these outrages and to allay the excitement, detachments of troops were posted for some time at Nadiad and other places in the district, but were not actively employed.

In Kaira district, 82 persons were sent up for trial of whom 17 were convicted. There were two sentences of transportation for life, the remaining sentences being rigorous imprisonment for periods varying from ten years to one-and-a-half months. 'According to the statement of the District Magistrate, Ahmedabad, a local levy was made in order to give compensation to those who had suffered from the destruction of property during the disorder. It was recovered in three different ways by levy from income-tax payees, by levy from the payees of the general municipal water-rate in Ahmedabad and also by confiscation of the caution-money of the mill-hands. The mill-hands always deposited one week's caution-money with the employers . . . This method of raising money was criticised as inequitable and putting an unfair burden on certain people. It does not appear to us that this was a measure taken to cope with the disturbances.'

The first outbreak in the Punjab occurred at Amritsar on the 10th April, 1919. It had a population of 1,50,000 and the most active and influential leaders—certainly in the period just before the disturbances—were Dr. Saifuddin Kitchlew and Dr. Satyapal. 'Their speeches', the committee reported, 'some of which we have examined and some of which afterwards came in question at their trial before a Tribunal established under martial law—show that on such points as the Rowlatt Bill, the expected Turkish Peace terms, and indeed on many if not all disputed matters, their attitude was one of very vigorous complaint against Government, In particular both of these gentlemen had joined Mr. Gandhi's Civil Disobedience Movement and had taken the *Satyagraha* vow to disobey the Rowlatt Act and any other laws which a committee should select.'

On 23 March a meeting was held in Amritsar in support of Gandhi's movement, and at another meeting on 29 March a *hartal* was decided on for the following day. On the same day, Dr. Satyapal was served with an order by the Punjab Government under the Defence of India Act, prohibiting him from speaking in public. The *hartals* on the 30th March and 6th April were successful and stopped the whole business in the city. Dr. Kitchlew was served with an order similar to that made against Dr. Satyapal.

'The Deputy Commissioner, Miles Irving, was much perturbed by the proof afforded by the second *hartal* and of the power and influence of Dr. Kitchlew and Satyapal. The Deputy Commissioner stated, 'Who are at the bottom of this I cannot say . . . Kitchlew himself I regard as the local agent of very much bigger men ... I think that things will be worse before they are better and that for the present we must rely on ourselves alone.'

The orders of the local government for the deportation of Dr. Kitchlew and Satyapal reached the Deputy Commissioner on the evening of the 9th April. They were to be removed quietly to Dharamsala. The Deputy Commissioner decided to send for the two leaders to his house on 10 April at 10 A.M. They were accompanied by some friends. In about half an hour, they had left for Dharamsala by motor car as arranged.

Soon after the news of the deportation was spreading in the city, shops were being closed and crowds were collecting. A huge crowd of people was much excited and angry and was making for civil lines, in order to see the Deputy Commissioner. The crowd was stopped by the mounted picket at the end of the Hall Bridge. The crowd pushed back the picket making the horses restive and uncontrollable by hitting them with sticks. The crowd resorted to stoning the men of the picket. Meanwhile crowds from Hathi Gate and Lohgarh Gate joined them. Now the number rose to about 30,000 persons. The committee reported, 'the non-commissioned officer incharge was given the necessary order, the crowd was fired upon and between twenty and thirty casualties ensued . . . At this stage, and of this crowd, we consider it certain that the temper and determination to violence was more obvious, more resolute and more vicious than that which had been exhibited earlier in the day. We think that the order to fire was rightly given and we can find no ground for saying that the necessity of the moment was in any way exceeded or abused.'

The committee recorded the murders, arson and loot by the crowd in Amritsar. At the National Bank, the Manager, Mr. Stewart and his assistant, Mr. Scott, were brutally beaten to death by the mob. Their bodies were burnt in a pile of bank furniture. The building was sacked, set on fire and completely gutted. The godowns at the rear in which large quantities of piece-goods were kept were broken into and thrown open for looting.[12] The Alliance Bank was also attacked and its Manager, G.M. Thomson who attempted to defend himself with a revolver was brutally murdered and flung from the balcony on to the street: his body was burnt in the street in a tragic manner under a huge pile of bank furniture drenched in kerosene oil. Similarly, at the Chartered Bank, glass and other property had been smashed and an attempt made to set it on fire. The mob was, however, dispersed by the police.

The committee reported, 'No steps whatever were taken to see what could be seen from the *Kotwali* or its immediate precincts, to get information about Hall Bazar from the gateway, to keep an eye on the crowds at the back of the Town Hall, to keep a lock-out in the direction of the Alliance Bank or any of the other banks which had been picketed on the *hartal* of the 6th. The Deputy Superintendent did not even receive a single report from the detectives who were his only scouts. His conduct at the Chartered Bank was pointless and ineffective beyond excuse ... It is not clear from his evidence that up to 1-30 he had done anything: It is clear that from that time until 5 o'clock he took no steps to make an enquiry or to do anything as regards the city or as regards his main reserve. He knew enough and more than enough to call for energetic action; the duty upon which he employed all his time and 25 of his armed men were idle and unnecessary after the first ten minutes; since the Europeans could have been brought at once to the *Kotwali* and a small picket left at the bank within hail of those headquarters.'[13]

Besides, there were other cases of arson, looting, damage to property and ghastly murders in Amritsar City. The whole telephone system was put out of action when the telephone instruments were smashed to pieces and the telephone exchange with its switchboard and fittings destroyed. The goods yard was stormed, damaged and looted and Guard Robinson of the North-Western Railway was chased and brutally beaten to death. Mr. Bennett, the station superintendent was caught and injured severely but the station picket saved his life. Besides, Sergeant Rowlands, an electrician in the military workers department, was attacked near the Rigo Bridge and was murdered.[14]

The mob also chased a lady missionary. Miss Sherwood, while she was bicycling in a narrow street in the city on her way to one of her schools. She was intercepted and overtaken while on the ground: when she got up to run she was knocked down again more than once; a door which she tried to enter was slammed in her face; in the end she was left on the street because she was thought to be dead.[15] Besides the Indian Christian Church and the Religious Book Society's Depot and Hall were burnt. The sub-post offices at the Golden Temple, Majith Mandi and Dhab Basti Ram were looted. At Bhagtanwala railway station which is on the Taran Taran line, the station was looted and burnt; the goods-shed and a wagon were looted; the point-locks and the telegraph wires were broken. At the night the Chheharta railway station was attacked by villagers who looted a goods train that was standing in the yard.

The committee clarified in its report, 'This narrative of mob violence while doubtless not exhaustive is sufficient to show the nature and character of the outbreak in all important respects. That it was anti-Government is clear at every stage: starting in anger at the action of Government in deporting the two local politicians[19] it proceeded by attack upon post offices and the railway . . . The attack upon the banks was primarily motivated by the race-hatred which led and directed the desire for destruction and loot. The records of the trial certainly go to show that the actual perpetrators of brutal murder were not representative Amritsar citizens but of what may be called the "hooligan" class; some of whom in Amritsar appear to have had a certain leadership or influence over those of their own kind . . . We do not omit to notice and to signalise the fact that some Indian citizens were doing their best to reason with crowds which had to be repulsed at Hall Bridge, that Miss Sherwood was ultimately taken care of by some Indians . . . Other efforts by sane and loyal citizens inside the city on that day we have no doubt there were.'[17]

The Commissioner of the Division, A.J.W. Kitchin and the Deputy Inspector-General of Police, D. Donald, arrived at the railway station from Lahore by motor car on the evening of the 10th April. The total number of persons killed on the 10th by the fire of the troops was approximately ten; the number wounded must be greater.

On the evening of the 11th April, Brigadier-General R.E.H. Dyer, who commanded a Brigade at Jullundur Cantonment, arrived at Amritsar and took over charge from Major Macdonald. He transferred the headquarters from the railway station to the Ram Bagh, a central place in the city. On the 12 April a strong column under General Dyer marched round the city as crowds were reported to be collected outside it. These were made to go back peaceably and the troops went into the city to the *Kotwali*. General Dyer deposed before the committee that the bearing of the local inhabitants was most insolent and many of them spat on the ground as the troops passed.[18]

On 13 April, General Dyer went through the city with the District Magistrate and some other officials and had a proclamation read by the *naib-tahsildar* to the people. From an examination of the map where the proclamation was read, it is evident that in many parts of the city the proclamation was not read. The committee reported that many people on hearing the proclamation[19] read did not treat it seriously, but that remarks were made that it was bluff, that General Dyer would not fire and not to be afraid. At the time when "General Dyer's proclamation was being read out, a counter-proclamation was made to the effect that the meeting was to be held in the afternoon in the Jallianwala Bagh. A meeting had been held a day earlier in the compound of the Hindu Sabha School at which an announcement had been made for a meeting to be held at the Jallianwala Bagh on the 13th April.'[19]

About one o'clock, General Dyer received the information that the people intended to hold a huge meeting at 4.30 P.M. On being asked why he did not take measures to prevent it being held, he replied, 'I went there as soon as I could. I had to think the matter out, I had to organise my forces and make up my mind as to where I might put my pickets. I thought I had done enough to make the crowd not meet. If they were going to meet, I had to consider the military situation and make up mind what to do, which took me a certain amount of time.'

About 4 o'clock in the afternoon of 13th April, the General received definite information that a meeting was being held at Jallianwala Bagh contrary to the terms of the proclamation issued by him earlier. He then proceeded through the city with a number of pickets which he left at pre-arranged places, and a special force of 25 Gorkhas and 25 Baluchis armed with rifles; 40 Gorkhas armed only with *Kukris* and two armoured cars. On arriving at Jallianwala Bagh, he entered with this force by a narrow entrance which was not sufficiently wide to allow the cars to pass. They were left in the street outside. 'According to the report sent by General Dyer to the Adjutant-General after the occurrence the crowd numbered about 6,000. It is probable that it was much more numerous and that from 10 to 20 thousand people were assembled.'

The committee stated, without giving the crowd any warning to disperse, which he considered unnecessary as they were in breach of his proclamation, he ordered his troops to fire and the firing was continued for about 10 minutes. There is no evidence as to the nature of the address to which the audience was listening. None of them was provided with firearms although some of them may have been carrying sticks.' As a result of this firing approximately 379 persons were killed. No figure was given for the wounded as their number may be taken as probably three times as great as the number of killed.'

The committee criticised the action of General Dyer thus: 'General Dyer's action in firing on the crowd at Jallianwala Bagh is open to criticism in two respects. *First,* that he started firing without giving the people who had assembled a chance to disperse, and *second* that he continued firing for a substantial period of time after the crowd had commenced to disperse.'

'In the ordinary case where a proclamation has been issued forbidding assemblies of people and intimating that a gathering held in defiance of the proclamation may have to be dispersed by military force, notice is properly given to the crowd before they are actually fired upon. The military situation at the time, *e.g.*, the risk of a small force of soldiers being overwhelmed by a threatening mob may justify firing without the formality of giving a notice to disperse, being observed. The only person who can judge whether or not such an emergency has arisen is the officer-in-command of the troops. In his report to the General Staff dated 25th August, 1919, General Dyer does not suggest the existence of such an emergency from anything observed by him in the demeanour of the crowd prior to his giving the order to fire. When examined before us he explained that his mind was made up as he came along in his motor car—if his orders against holding a meeting were disobeyed he was going to fire at once. Apparently, he looked upon the warning which he had given in the morning as sufficient notice and justification for his firing upon a crowd assembling in defiance thereof.

'The majority at all events of the people who assembled had done so in direct defiance of a proclamation issued in the interests of peace and order—many thinking that the reference to firing was mere bluff. In spite of this circumstance notice to disperse would have offered those assembled in ignorance of the proclamation and other people also an opportunity to leave the Bagh and should have been given. If the notice had been disregarded, General Dyer would have been justified in firing on the crowd, to compel it to disperse.

'In continuing to fire as he did it appears to us that General Dyer committed a grave error ... In continuing firing as long as he did, it is evident that General Dyer had in view not merely the dispersal of the crowd that had assembled contrary to his orders, but the desire to produce a moral effect in the Punjab ... In our view this was unfortunately a mistaken conception of his duty. If necessary a crowd that has assembled contrary to a proclamation issued to prevent or terminate disorder may have to be fired upon; but continued firing upon the crowd cannot be justified because of the effect such firing may have upon people in other places. The employment of excessive measures is as likely as not to produce the opposite result to that desired.

'The action taken by General Dyer has also been described by others as having saved the situation in the Punjab and having averted a rebellion on a scale similar to the Mutiny. It does not, however, appear to us possible to draw this conclusion, particularly in view of the fact that it is not proved that a conspiracy to overthrow British power had been formed, prior to outbreaks.'

The committee viewed the situation in Amritsar thus: 'It is quite true that in the course of the 12th the position was hardening into *de facto* martial law. The Commissioner had left on the night of the 11th and General Dyer had arrived somewhat later on that night. On the 13th formal martial law was expected; the telegram sanctioning it was dispatched at midnight; the trouble had been spreading and Amritsar was known not to be the only area involved. The proclamation of the 13th imposed permits for travel and a curfew at 8 P.M.; it prohibited gatherings or processions. These were not unreasonable orders in themselves; they were issued with the cognizance of the Deputy Commissioner; had they been widely enforced little would have been heard of any special grievance over this single day.'[20]

The disturbances in the district of Lahore occurred first in the town of Lahore and then in the Kasur sub-division. The committee recorded that trouble in the capital had been brewing for some time before it eventuated in serious disorder on the evening of the 10th April. The disorders in Kasur occurred on the 12th, no marked premonitory signs having preceded it in that locality.

In Lahore, an active opposition to the Rowlatt Bills had started very early after their publication in the *Gazette of India* on the 18th January, 1919. The protest meetings were held on 4 February and 9 March at the Bradlaugh Hall under the leadership of Lala Duni Chand, Dr. Saifuddin Kitchlew and Rambhaj Dutt. On 18 March, Rowlatt Bill No. 2 was passed and this was followed on 24 March by Gandhi's call for a *hartal,* a twenty-four hours' fast, cessation from work and the holding of public meetings. The *hartal* of the 6th April was complete. Processions were taken out.[21] The committee stated in its report, 'Thus although no collision between the people and the police took place, there were, from the point of view of the authorities, very disquieting elements in the day's occurrences and the police had a strenuous time. For the most part shopkeepers closed their shops voluntarily but there were certain cases where coercion was employed against people who wished to keep their shops open and against people riding in cars. The crowds marching through the streets indulged in cries such as *Hai Hai George Mar Gya* (King George is dead). They demonstrated against Indians who were believed to be friendly to the Government. At the meeting in the Bradlaugh Hall, European police officers who attended were loudly hooted and hissed. ... It may be noted that resolutions were passed condemning the authorities at Delhi for having fired upon innocent persons without any justification and viewing with alarm and disapproval the orders passed by the Punjab Government against Dr. Kitchlew, Satyapal and others.'[22]

On 10 April the political atmosphere, already highly charged, was made acutely worse with the arrival of the news that Gandhi had been prohibited from entering the Punjab and Dr. Kitchlew and Dr. Satyapal had been deported. Crowds had begun to assemble in the city, shops were closed and shouts of *Mahatma Gandhi Ki Jai* were heard. Students made themselves prominent with their participation with the demonstrators. When the crowd reached the Mall, it became out of control.

On 11 April, the shops in the city were closed and a huge crowd of Hindus and Muslims—numbering about 25,000—collected in the Badshahi Mosque. This crowd was addressed by Rambhaj Dutt and others. Inside the gate of the mosque, a banner was hung bearing the inscription, 'the king who practises tyranny cuts his own roots underneath.' Inflammatory speeches were delivered in the course of which allegations were made that the police had fifed on the crowd the preceding day after they, had retreated and that this action was a tyrannical action.

The committee observed thus, 'At the conclusion of the meeting, the mob headed by hooligans carrying sticks marched through the city shouting. On the way, they destroyed pictures of the King Emperor and the Queen Empress shouting that "King George is dead." The band of hooligans referred to was known as the *Danda Fauj*.[23] They went about the city in a band on the 11th and 12th, their leader delivering seditious lectures in the bazaar saying the King George was not their king, that the Amir of Afghanistan and the Emperor of Germany were their kings. They carried sticks after the manner of troops with rifles and recruited supporters from the mobs. Apart from these crude manifestations of sedition which took place after the meeting, the meeting itself was a very extraordinary one to be held in a mosque.'[24]

By this time, the authorities resolved to regain control over the city with a mixed column of 800 police and military personnel under Colonel Frank Johnson who entered the city by the Delhi Gate. This force was supported by two aeroplanes and in case the troops on the march should be bombed or fired upon from the houses. The crowds appeared and strong forces of Indian troops and police were posted in the city. When the column got to the Hira Mandi, there was a large crowd moving to and from the Badshahi Mosque. Some of them were armed with *lathis*. This crowd took no notice of any warnings to disperse and eventually a Muhammadan magistrate was sent to clear the mosque. This he did and crowds came out of it. Cavalry tried to disperse them, but they refused to go and attempted to stampede the horses. Eventually a dense mass collected at the Hira Mandi where there was a considerable open space. Stone-throwing began and the police had to fire. One man was killed and 28 were wounded. 'We think that it was essential on this day to disperse this crowd and that it would have been the end of all chance to restore order in Lahore if the police and troops had left without dispersing it.'

Several posters of a seditious and inflammatory character which had been exhibited in different parts of the city were secured by the police. Some of them were issued on either dates than the 10th. For example, on 6th April a poster was removed from the Bradlaugh Hall in which it was said, 'To practise tyranny and to give it the name of love, what a fine trick is this of the civilisation of the West.' Of the posters appearing on the 12th the committee referred to one containing such passages as these: 'We are the Indian nation whose bravery and honour have been acknowledged by all the kings of the world. The English are the worst lot and are like monkeys whose deceit and cunning are obvious to all, high and low. Have these monkeys forgotten their original conditions? Now these faithless people have forgotten the loyalty of Indians, are bent upon exercising limitless tyranny. O brethren, gird up your loins and fight. Kill and be killed. Do not lose courage and try your utmost to turn those mean monkeys from your holy country.'[25]

Soon after, pre-censorship was imposed upon all local newspapers. On 13 April, the district of Lahore was proclaimed under the Seditious Meetings Act and notice was given forbidding all assemblies of more than ten persons. Besides liquor shops were ordered to close.

At Kasur, the *hartal* was observed on 12 April, 1919 and a huge crowd under the leadership of Nadir Ali Shah took its way to the railway station carrying a *charpoy* with a black flag on it by way of symbolising the 'funeral of liberty'. It did considerable damage by breaking doors and throwing stones at windows. The instruments at the telegraph office were put out of action, furniture was set on fire, the booking office ransacked, an oil-shed was burnt, the telegraph wires were cut and all the goods inside the station buildings were looted or destroyed.

The committee also referred to the incident of the attack of the mob on Captain Limby and Lieutenant Munro who were greeted with shouts of 'kill them, kill them'. With difficulty they managed to fight their way along the side of the train and sought refuge in a village. 'It is hardly doubtful that if they had been overpowered their lives would have been taken.' At one stage, when the mob was out of control, police resorted to fire. As a result of it, four men died and a few were wounded. The committee stated, 'We uphold the decision to fire upon the mob and think that it should have been fired upon before the Deputy Superintendent of Police arrived.' On 12 April troops arrived from Ferozepur and further trouble was thus averted. On 16 April martial law was imposed at Kasur.

On 12 April the railway station at Khem Karan[26] was attacked by a 'gang' of about twenty-five persons. Some damage was done to the telegraph apparatus and some articles were looted, but the rioters were driven off by the police.

A very serious outbreak occurred at Gujranwala.[27] On 5 April, 1919, a meeting was held at which resolutions were passed disapproving of the Rowlatt Bills. On 14 April, crowds had been astir; forcing shopkeepers to close their shops; shouting against the Rowlatt Bills and uttering *'jais'* for Hindu-Muslim unity and for various well-known leaders. A huge crowd assembled at the railway station when a train from Lahore had arrived. They tried to prevent passengers from going to Wazirabad for the *Baisakhi* fair there. The driver and the guard were interfered with and the train was stoned. It moved out of the station with an excited crowd following it. Besides, the Katchi bridge had been set on fire by piling wood soaked in petroleum upon the sleepers. The telegraph wires had been cut on both sides of Gujranwala. Meetings were addressed about the Rowlatt Act. The city post office was burnt and water-pumps were damaged. The crowds were waving back flags and hurling bricks. The *tahsil*, the church, the *dak* bungalow and the district courts were all set on fire. The police lines were also attacked. The mob returned to the railway station, set the buildings and the goods-shed on fire and looted the property.[28]

When the police were nearly exhausted, three aeroplanes from Lahore arrived over the town. Major Carberry first took action outside the town of Gujranwala. He dropped, as he reported to the committee, three bombs on a party of about 150 persons who were making for Gujranwala. This was outside a village two miles away from the town. A woman and a boy were killed and two men slightly wounded. Meanwhile, Major Carberry observed a party of about 200 persons in the field near the Khalsa High School and Boarding House. He dropped a bomb which burst in a courtyard and several persons were wounded. Thirty rounds were fired at the party with the machine gun. 'We were informed that so far as is known the casualties on this occasion were one man hit by a splinter and one small boy stunned.' Of the other two aeroplanes sent to Gujranwala from Lahore, one took no action; the other fired 25 rounds from its machine-gun upon a gathering of 20 to 30 persons on a level crossing between the civil lines and the city, but dropped no bombs.

The committee reported, 'Colonel O'Brien, the Deputy Commissioner of Gujranwala informed us that so far as could be ascertained the total casualties in Gujranwala on 14th April including those killed by bombs and machine-guns and those shot by the police were 11 killed and 27 wounded'.[29]

The committee gave its final verdict thus: 'It appears to us that in the circumstances the decision to use bomb-carrying aeroplanes at Gujranwala on the 14th April was justified . . .

The rioters had cut off communication by telegraph or telephone between Gujranwala and outside places; they had been trying their best to make the railway useless for sending troops to the town; their violence could only be measured when it had been stopped; it was not stopped till the aeroplanes appeared, the police had definitely failed to impose control and were practically exhausted . . . We are not prepared to lay down as a charter for rioters that when they succeed in preventing the ordinary resources of Government from being utilised to suppress them they are to be exempt from having to reckon with such resources as remain ... As regards the bombs which fell in Gujranwala, we confine ourselves to the two bombs which burst. This action we uphold. These bombs appear to have fallen in the midst of rioters caught in the act of rioting and fully minded to continue . . . These bombs were not only justified, but in our view, were invaluable, and the fact that the disorders were ended by the aeroplanes long before troops arrived, is, we think in large measure attributable to them . . . Major Carberry's action in firing with his machine-guns upon crowds in the streets of Gujranwala does not appear to us excessive. He explained to us that there was a large crowd and these rounds were fired as people who were collecting round the station and who were running away when they saw him begin to fire. It is no doubt difficult to judge from a flying machine moving rapidly in the air, the moment at which effective and definite dispersal of a large crowd has been ensured.

'The instructions which should be given to officers in charge of aeroplanes when employed in the suppression of disorders might appropriately form the subject of a careful inquiry by those in command of the Air Force. Special problems are presented in the use both of bombs and of machine-guns from the air and there may be other means with which an aeroplane might be provided for dispersing crowds.'[20]

The disorder spread extensively in the Gujranwala district. These places were Wazirabad, Akalgarh and Hafizabad. Renewed acts of disorder occurred on 15th April. Persistent attacks were made upon the railway. The rails about one-and-a-half miles from Dhahan Singh Station were torn up and telegraph wires cut. The station itself was attacked and looted. The arrival of the armoured train marked the end of disorder.

In Gujrat city, Jalalpur Jattan and Malakwal crowds of people had black-flag demonstrations. *Hartal* was observed, railway furniture was damaged and telegraph wires were cut. The police controlled the situation and there was no casualty.

In Lyallpur, the local Congress committee gave a call for *hartal* which was successfully observed without any incident. The committee reported, 'During this period a very disquieting and prominent feature in Lyallpur was the continued exhibition of posters of an inflammatory and criminal character . . . On the 13th and 14th, nothing occurred save excited and noisy gathering of people, but the tension was such that on the evening of the 14th all the Europeans (the number was about 907) were concentrated in two bungalows in the Civil Lines so that they might more easily be defended. . . In the night of the 17th, four out of eight stacks of Government fefcuia[31] at the station were burnt. No one was ever sent up for trial or convicted for this though the damage done amounted to about ₹ 50,000 and it seems just possible that it caught fire accidentally. More troops arrived on the 17th and on the 19th, a movable column came to Lyallpur. its presence safeguarding the town against further disorder.'

The committee gave its findings about the attacks on means of communication operated by the government. The interruptions of the telegraph and railways were persistent and widespread. This was one of the earliest manifestations of violence in Amritsar on 10 April and 'the earliest date at which we can put its cessation in the Punjab is the 22nd April.'[32] Such attacks were motivated by sheer anti-government feeling. The Railway considered a government institution and railway damage was in these cases simply a part of the destruction of government property which the mobs had burnt. There was an additional motive to prevent the arrival of troops and to make calls for assistance impossible.

'After the 10th April the railway staff in all its various classes were interfered with by people inciting them to stay away from their work and molesting them on the way to their duties. On the 12th a large proportion of the men in the locomotive shops failed to present themselves. At Shakurpur, the locomotive, carriage, wagon and traffic staff struck work on the 13th ... This strike spread to Delhi-Kishanganj just outside the Punjab.... At Ambala there was a short strike of the traffic staff, but this was not very serious. These facts are sufficient to illustrate the reality of the apprehension that disorders arising among the general public would combine, with special grievances on the part of railway employees, to precipitate a strike not in one department only, but in many, which might for a time paralyse the railway system.'[33]

During the period of unrest, passenger trains were in general got through, though very late. The goods traffic suffered more, and in the disturbed areas, the railway as a commercial system was practically paralysed between 10 and 21 April. Derailment of trains was resorted to by the rioters in some cases. In one case an armoured train was derailed by a mob having removed the joints and opened out the rails. A rail was removed at Kala, near Jhelum and a passenger train was derailed. 'In view of the difficulties in running the traffic and also for reasons of policy which weighed with both the military and the civil authorities, passenger traffic was severely restricted for a time, especially after the 14th April.

The committee also gave details about the causes of these disturbances in its report. These were the arrests and deportations of Dr. Saifuddin Kitchlew and Dr. Satyapal, Home Rule Movement and its self-determination principles, promulgation of Defence of India Act, post-war problems, Rowlatt Bills, passive resistance, civil disobedience campaign, all-India *hartals* on 30 March, 6 April and Gandhi's arrest. 'In the situation as it presented itself day by day to the Punjab Government, there were grounds for the gravest anxiety . . . Apart from the existence of any deeply laid scheme to overthrow the British, a movement which had started in rioting and became a rebellion might have rapidly developed into a revolution.'

The application of martial law and its necessity under the existing circumstances in the Punjab was also dealt with by the committee. 'It is a question of fact, and on the information submitted to us, we think that the answer should be given in the affirmative. . . 'Open rebellion', we think, apt and accurate; as a question of inference it appears to us to be the natural and the only inference.'

'The Amritsar incidents may be regarded as the high water mark of the disorders, though the outbreak at Kasur on the 12th is hardly distinguishable. Gujranwala on the 14th exhibits the same anti-Government features . . . The acts of the mob at Lahore upon the 10th were less serious, but the occurrence there between the 10th and the 13th show an equally marked defiance of constituted authority and a direct relation with the Amritsar outbreak . . . Where the Government is British and a comparatively insignificant number of the inhabitants, are Europeans, most of them Government servants, and this intention is seen to eliminate at prominent points in a murderous attack on Europeans simply as such, it may be said with some certainty that the Government so attacked is in face of an open rebellion in all reasonable implications of the phrase.'[34]

As regards the extension of martial law to Gujrat and Lyallpur districts, the committee opined, 'In neither district were the actual outbreaks so serious as in the others and in both it is clear that disturbances were spreading in imitation of or by contagion from Amritsar and Gujranwala. The form which seemed to spread most easily and which threatened to become the gravest was the attack upon the telegraphs and railway.

'Under Regulation X of 1804, we do not find that the discretion given to the Governor-General-in-Council is restricted, when open rebellion has broken out in part of the territories under his jurisdiction, so as to limit by any technical considerations other than those of expediency and sound policy the area over which martial law may be proclaimed. In our opinion the situation which had arisen in the Punjab was one of extreme gravity and the authorities were justified in declaring martial law and partially suspending the ordinary tribunals in the different districts to which martial law was applied.'[35]

As regards martial law orders and cases arising out of the breach thereof, the committee opined that in several important respects martial law assumed an intensive form. 'It was not being administered in any enemy country but in a country where, on the restoration of normal conditions it was advisable that martial law administration should leave behind as little feeling of bitterness and unfairness as possible. Some of the orders issued were injudicious. They served no good purpose and were not, in our opinion, drawn with sufficient tact to prevent undue annoyance to the civil population.'

The most criticised of these orders was probably, what had come to be known as General Dyer's crawling order. The committee was critical of such an inhuman order affecting directly the honour and dignity of a common Indian. It, therefore, observed, 'The order is certainly open to the objection that it caused unnecessary inconvenience to a number of people and that it unnecessarily punished innocent as well as guilty. Above all, from an administrative point of view in subjecting the Indian population to an act of humiliation, it has continued to be a cause of bitterness and racial ill-feeling long after it was recalled.'

Another order open to similar objection was the *salaaming* order pronounced by General Campbell on 22 April, 1919. This order was as follows: 'Where it has come to my notice that certain inhabitants of the Gujranwala District are habitually exhibiting a lack of respect for gazetted or commissioned European Civil and Military Officers of His Majesty's Service thereby failing to maintain the dignity of that Government. I hereby order that the inhabitants of the Gujranwala District shall accord to all such officers, whenever met, the salutation usually accorded to Indian gentlemen of high social position in accordance with the customs of India. That is to say persons riding on animals or in wheeled conveyance will alight, persons carrying opened and raised umbrellas shall lower them, and all persons shall salute or *salaam* with the hand.' The committee had a word of criticism for such an order, 'It may be right that during the administration of martial law all the civilian population should *salaam* or salute officers of His Majesty's Services. The marks of respect, however, mentioned in the order which were shown by social inferiors to their social superiors are practically no longer in observance. No good object was served by making all Indians whatever their station, show these signs of respect to all Commissioned Officers.'

The infliction of sentences of flogging by area officers for offences committed against martial law orders was subject to criticism in some respects. When martial law was declared, triangles or whipping posts were set up in Amritsar near the Fort and at some other places in the city. The Committee opined, 'We are of opinion that even under martial law administration, no flogging should take place in public.'

The members of the committee who gave the minority report, thought that in Delhi a difficult situation was handled with tact and restraint by the Chief Commissioner. In Ahmedabad, the Collector dealt with a sudden and grave outburst of mob fury with discretion and judgment. 'In Ahmedabad, where the atrocities committed by the unruly mob were as bad as those at Amritsar. Martial Law was never proclaimed, only one or two orders which were considered necessary by the military authorities for restoration of order were issued and remained in force only for two days and nothing was done savouring of a desire to punish the whole population or to teach them a lesson for the events of the 10th and 11th April. Ahmedabad was the birthplace of *Satyagraha* Movement with the offshoot of civil disobedience and intensive propaganda was carried on in the districts of Ahmedabad and Kaira but no repressive measures were undertaken.'[36]

The members did not agree in the view that the riots in the Punjab were in the nature of a rebellion. To suggest that they had the elements of a revolution and might have rapidly developed into one was an exaggerated view of the events which was not justified.

About the mob activity and the firing at Amritsar, the committee stated, 'With regard to the events at Amritsar, we are unable to hold that the crowd as they were going over the bridge, and before they had been fired upon or turned back, were crying out, 'where is the Deputy Commissioner? We will butcher him to pieces.'[37]

'We think it is not correct to say that the firing was in no sense the cause of the excesses on the 10th April. The excesses committed by the mob on that day were altogether inexcusable and nothing that had happened afforded any justification for them. But on the evidence before us, we think that it is true that the crowds, when they started to go to the Deputy Commissioner and came on the bridge, had no intention of committing any excesses. After the firing they lost their heads and seized by a mad frenzy started on their nefarious work. This is supported by the statement of Mr. Miles Irving.'[38]

The committee gave its verdict on the question whether these events were in the nature of a rebellion as commonly understood, that is, a rising for the purpose of turning out the British Government and were the result of an organised movement for that end. On the basis of the evidence, the dissenting members stated that there was no rebellion of any kind nor any organisation for that purpose. Besides, there was no organisation even for bringing about the disturbances and the atrocities which are committed by the mobs seized by the frenzy of the moment. 'The Punjab Government in their case presented to us take the view that the disturbances cannot be rightly attributed to an organisation for that purpose, but must be referred mainly to local causes . . . Speaking about Amritsar where the worst disorders took place, the Punjab Government say, "that certain local factors resulted in turning what started as a protest in force against the deportation of Drs. Kitchlew and Satyapal into mob-violence marked by murder, pillage and incendiarism."

At Lahore, the disturbances followed the reported arrest of Mahatma Gandhi and the news of outrages at Amritsar. At Gujranwala, the actual disorder was due rather to the desire to emulate the outrages of the mob at Lahore and Amritsar rather than to any long premeditated organisation for violent ends. Similarly, at Kasur, Gujrat and other places, the record of the disturbances disclosed no evidence of any kind of political organization wedded to the cult of violence.

Similarly, the conclusion arrived at by an investigation conducted by the police chief of Delhi clarified the disputed point of rioting by a mob in the city. He stated that the rioting in Delhi was not the outcome of a conspiracy against the British *Raj*, but it was the natural consequence of economic hardships and political unrest. He further said that it was never intended by the members of the *Satyagraha Sabha* or others that their activities should result in violence. He added that he could find no connection between the Delhi disturbances and the disturbances in other places.

'The marked differences as regards certain essential features in the disturbances at different places also negative any common design. While in Amritsar and Ahmedabad the mobs, when they lost self-control and started on their nefarious work, brutally assaulted and killed Europeans and destroyed Government and public property, it was quite otherwise in Lahore and Delhi. During the disturbed time of the 10th of April and the following days, there was no determined attempt at Lahore to molest Europeans or attack banks or public buildings. Similarly, in Delhi, throughout the period of the disturbances from the 30th March to the 17th April, there was never any attempt made to damage Government or public buildings or any attack on Europeans as such.'[39]

To prove their contention that it was not a rebellion, the dissenting members opined that in no place were the mobs provided with any fire-arms or swords or other weapons of that character. At no time was any attempt made by the crowds to obtain arms by raiding the houses of licence-holders or the ammunition shops in the disturbed areas'.[40] In several cases, in the beginning of the disturbances, people had not come armed even with *lathis* or sticks.

At Amritsar, when the crowd first started to go to the Deputy Commissioner's bungalow, they were bare-headed and bare-footed and had no sticks in their hands. It was after they had been turned back by the firing that some of them armed themselves with sticks and pieces of wood from a shop near the railway station.

Moreover, no serious attempt appeared to have been made to involve the rural population to join the disturbances. The official evidence was unanimous that the rural population, as a whole, had nothing to do with these disturbances. In fact, Lt. Colonel Smithers who had been commanding a mobile column for the maintenance of law and order, happened to visit various areas in the Lahore district and reported thus to General Beynon, 'My impression as regards the loyalty of the district was that outside the larger towns the country folk seemed contented. They were at the time busy in cutting their crops and did not appear interested in anything else. Most outlying villages had not even heard of the Rowlatt Bill. I never heard Lahore mentioned in the district I traversed except that they had heard of riots there.'[41]

To strengthen their point of view the dissenting members argued that the anti-government or anti-British form the disturbances took was a sudden development at the time. The Punjab government testified to the fact that on the 30th March; and 6th April, when the *hartal* took place and on the 9th April; which was the *Ram Naumi* day, there was no hostility or even discourtesy shown at Amritsar to Europeans who could move freely in the town. Besides, it was not correct to say that at Gujranwala, Kasur and other places, the violent acts committed by the mob were more or less the result of a sudden determination to resort to such acts. In the town of Lahore itself the actual happenings in the way of destruction of life and property were of so trivial a character that it would be a misnomer to describe them as acts of rebellion. In fact, there was no damage done to any property, government or private, and there was no attempt to attack Europeans as such.

The dissenting members had a word of criticism in connection with the promulgation of martial law in the Punjab. According to them the introduction of martial law as a preventive measure was not justified. In fact, there was not much fear of the recrudescence of the disturbances which were short-lived and the prevailing situation was well in hand and was capable, of being dealt with without taking the extreme step of introducing martial law. The speedy trial and punishment of offenders, could have been secured by other means and could not be a. sufficient justification for introducing martial law.

'To suggest; that martial law may be introduced as a punitive measure was, on the face of it, indefensible.

The dissenting members severely indicted General Dyer and his action in Jallianwala Bagh. 'General Dyer wanted by his action at Jallianwala Bagh to create a wide impression and a great moral effect. We have no doubt that he did succeed in creating a very wide impression and a great moral effect, but of a character quite opposite to the one he intended. The story of innocent people not engaged in any acts of violence but assembled in a meeting, has undoubtedly produced such a deep impression throughout the length and breadth of the country, so prejudicial to the British Government that it would take a good deal and a long time to rub it out. The action of General Dyer as well as some acts of the martial law administration. . . have been compared to the acts of "frightfulness" committed by some of the German military Commanders during the war in Belgium and France.

'General Dyer thought that he had crushed the rebellion and Sir Michael O'Dwyer was of the same view. There was no rebellion which required to be crushed. We feel that General Dyer by adopting an inhuman and un-British method of dealing with subjects of His Majesty the King-Emperor, has done great disservice to the interest of British Rule in India. This aspect it was not possible for the people of the mentality of General Dyer to realise.'[42]

The bombing of some areas in Gujranwala and the machinegunning of innocent people there was another point of indictment by the dissenting members. 'We are of opinion that looking to the inherent difficulties in regulating the operations of an aeroplane on a town, consisting of a large number of innocent people, the danger of a person in the aeroplane unfamiliar with the town not being able to make out unmistakably whether any particular people are peacefully engaged or otherwise and the consequent risk of hurting innocent people, are So grave that the use of aeroplanes in case of such disturbances is to be deprecated.'[43]

The 'fancy punishments' awarded to people at Kasur by Captain Doveton did not escape the notice of the dissenting members.[44] In a number of cases, he ordered people to be taken to the goods-shed to load and unload bales for a day or two. In the case of those who were so ordered to work for a day, they were allowed to go home for the night on depositing some of the belongings as security for their returning the next morning. 'We think this, in effect, amounted to rigorous imprisonment while they were so at work in the goods shed.'

The dissenting members criticised the way people were arrested and tried under martial law. People were arrested on mere suspicion and kept in custody for considerable periods. Some of them were never brought to trial and others brought before the court had to be discharged because there was absolutely no evidence against them. The members considered it a very unsatisfactory feature that people were kept for many days under arrest without being brought before a court and remanded, and facilities for bail were unnecessarily curtailed, even with regard to bailable offences.

The sentences passed by the martial law commissions were considerably reduced by government. Out of 108 death sentences, only 23 were maintained and the remaining were commuted to transportation in some cases, and in the rest to sentences of imprisonment going down to one year. Out of 265 sentences of transportation, only 2 were maintained, 5 were commuted altogether and the rest were commuted to imprisonments varying from one year to ten years. The members were critical of the system which operated with regard to these sentences. They stated, 'There is a great disproportion between the original sentences and those to which they were commuted and this gives ground for the suggestion of initial severity that has been made.'

REFERENCES

1. On 13 November, 1919, H.G. Stokes resigned on account of his ill-health, and on 24 November, H. Williamson, a senior police official, was appointed to succeed him as secretary.
2. See the resolution of the Government of India, Home Department, dated 14 October, 1919, in the preface, *Disorders Inquiry Committee Report, 1919-20,* Calcutta, 1920.
3. *Disorders Inquiry Committee Report*, pp. 1-142 and 145-236.

4. *Ibid.*, pp. 1-3.
5. *Ibid.*, pp. 3-4.
6. *Ibid.*, p. 6.
7. *Ibid.*, p. 8.
8. *Ibid.*, pp. 12-13.
9. Officer in Charge of revenue collection in a sub-division of a district.
10. *Disorders Inquiry Committee Report*, pp. 18-19.
11. Madhavlal, a revenue official, was burnt alive with kerosene oil by the mob.
12. *Disorders Inquiry Committee Report,* p. 35.
13. *Ibid.*, p. 37.
14. His skull was battered in apparently by a straining screw.
15. The assault has not been detailed by an eye-witness.
16. They were Dr. Saifuddin Kitchlew and Dr. Satyapal.
17. *Disorders Inquiry Committee Report*, pp. 39-40.
18. *Ibid.*, p. 42.
19. '. . . Any person found in the streets after 8 p.m. are liable to be shot. No procession of any kind is permitted to parade the streets in the city...
20. *Disorders Inquiry Committee Report,* p. 50.
21. Anarkali and the Mall witnessed huge processions.
22. *Disorders Inquiry Committee Report*, pp. 54-55.
23. Bludgeon army.
24. *Disorders Enquiry Committee Report*, pp. 58-59.
25. *Ibid.*, pp. 60-61.
26. A town situated eight miles away from Kasur.
27. Situated at a distance of 36 miles from Lahore; its population was 30,000.
28. *Disorders Inquiry Committee Report*, pp. 70 ff.
29. *Ibid.*
30. *Ibid.*
31. Cattle fodder.
32. The Director, Telegraph Engineering, Northern Circle, reported that between 10 April and 21 April, 1919 there were fifty-four such outrages.
33. *Disorders Inquiry Committee Report*, pp. 90-91.
34. *Ibid.*, pp. 108-109.

35. *Ibid.*, p. 118.
36. *Ibid.*, p. 145.
37. The allegation rested only on the testimony of Jiwan Lai, Inspector, Criminal Investigation Department. The committee did not rely on this evidence in the absence of any corroborative evidence.
38. *Disorders Inquiry Committee Report*, p. 147.
39. *Ibid.*, p. 157.
40. Lt. Colonel Johnson told the committee that there were 1709 licence holders in Lahore. The question was put to him, 'Am I right in supposing that if the people of these provinces had been bent on rebellion that (possessing arms) would have been the first thing they would have done? His answer was, 'I say that is my opinion. I think you are right.'
41. *Disorder Inquiry Committee Report*, pp. 157-158.
42. *Ibid.*, pp. 193-94.
43. *Ibid.*, p. 224.
44. These punishments are referred in the majority report.

Chapter 5
Public Opinion

The leaders of the Indian National Congress did not expect a true picture of the gruesome tragedy at Jallianwala Bagh and the atrocities perpetrated on people after the promulgation of martial law in the Punjab.[1] They, therefore, appointed a committee on 14 November, 1919 and its members were M.K. Gandhi, Motilal Nehru, Fazlul Haq, C.R. Das and Abbas Tyabji, and K. Santanam was the secretary. They were to examine, sift, collate and analyse the evidence already collected by and on behalf of the sub-committee regarding the tragic events which occurred in April 1919 in some of the districts of the Punjab, and to supplement such evidence, where necessary, and thus to present their conclusions.[2]

The Congress Committee entered upon their work on 17 November, 1919 and concluded their findings on 20 February, 1910. They examined the statements of over 1700 witnesses and selected for publication about 650 statements. Every admitted statement was verified by one of them and was accepted only after they were satisfied as to the *bona fides* of the witnesses. It is evident that some of the witnesses had made a very serious allegations against officials. 'In each and every case the witnesses were warned by us of the consequences of making those allegations and they were admitted only when the [witnesses adhered to their statements, in spite of the knowledge of the risk they personally ran and the damage that may [ensue to the cause by reason of exaggeration or untruth. We have, moreover, rejected those statements which could not be corroborated, although in some cases we were inclined to believe the witnesses.

Such, for instance, were the statements regarding ill-treatment of women.'

This inquiry was confined to the martial law excesses and the principal places covered in the report were Lahore, Amritsar, Taran Taran, Kasur, Gujranwala, Wazirabad, Chuharkana, Lyallpur, Gujrat, Malakwal and Sargodha. The Commissioners made use of the evidence led before the Disorders Inquiry Committee. Majority of the statements were given in the vernaculars which were translated later on. They also studied the records of the trials by martial law or summary courts.

The committee dealt with the nature of administration set up under Michael O'Dwyer in Punjab since his appointment as Lieutenant-Governor in 1913. He signalled his rule by 'contemptuous' references to proposals for reforms. It was followed by action under the Press Act. Security was demanded from several vernacular newspapers and the security already deposited was forfeited in some cases. He 'abused' the powers given to him by the Defence of India Act and interned hundreds of local men with little or no cause.

'As I proceeded further and further with my inquiry into the atrocities', Gandhi wrote in his *Autobiography*, 'that had been committed on the people, I came across tales of Government's tyranny and the arbitrary despotism of its officers such as I was hardly prepared for, and they filled me with deep pain. What surprised me then, and what still continues to fill me with surprise, was the fact that a province, that had. furnished the largest number of soldiers to the British Government during the war, should have taken all these brutal excesses lying down.'[3]

About the Congress report, Gandhi has given an objective assessment. 'All that I wish to say here about it is that there is not a single conscious exaggeration in it anywhere, and every statement made in it is substantiated by evidence. Moreover, the evidence published was only a fraction of what was in the Committee's possession. Not a single statement, regarding the validity of which there was the slightest room for doubt, was permitted to appear in the report. This report, prepared as it was solely with a view to bringing out the truth, and nothing but the truth, will enable the reader to see to what lengths the British Government is capable of going, and, what inhumanities and barbarities it is capable of perpetrating in order to maintain its power. So far as I am aware, not a single statement made in this report, has ever been disproved.'[4]

Jawaharlal Nehru narrated in his *Autobiography* thus: 'Deshbandhu Das especially took the Amritsar area under his charge and 1 was deputed to accompany him there and assist him in any way he desired. That was the first occasion I had of working with him and under him and I valued that experience very much and my admiration for him grew. Most of the evidence relating to Jallianwala Bagh and that terrible lane where human beings were made to crawl on their bellies, that subsequently appeared in the Congress Inquiry Report, was taken down in our presence. We paid numerous visits to the so-called Bagh itself and examined every bit of it carefully.'[5]

The Congress Committee reported that, 'All this popular demonstration and unfoldment of national consciousness would have gladdened any ruler with imagination and sympathy with popular aspirations. It only enraged Sir Michael O Dwyer. He was angry that his order...instead of cowing down the people, had only made them bolder and more articulate in their demands. Therefore, practically at the same time that the popular demonstration was going on in an orderly, perfectly constitutional manner, an order was being forged in the Punjab Government Secretariat which was to destroy and disturb the people's peace; for the Lieutenant-Governor had decided to deport Dr. Kitchlew and Satyapal.

The provocation given by the deportation of their beloved leaders to the people of Amritsar was grave and uncalled for. This was doubled when the unarmed crowd was prevented from proceeding on its peaceful errand, and upon becoming insistent was fired on ... It is difficult to say what would have happened, if the mob had been allowed to proceed to the Deputy Commissioner's bungalow and there had its prayer rejected as it was likely to be. It would have largely depended on the way the Deputy Commissioner dealt with them. It must be granted that the crowd was in an assertive mood, and if the authorities thought that the crowd would have acted in a violent manner, we are not prepared to blame for checking its advance. Our study of the evidence led before the Martial Law Commissions, of the official evidence led before Lord Hunter's Committee and the evidence collected by us, leads to the conclusion that there was no warrant for the firing. The authorities omitted all the intermediate stages that are usually resorted in all civilised countries. There was no parleying, no humouring and no use of milder force. Immediately the crowd became insistent, the order to fire was given. In this country, it has become too much the custom with the executive and the military never to run any risk, or to put it in another way, to count Indian life very cheap."[6]

The adverse comments against the inactivity and vacillation shown by the police force posted at the *Kotwali* police station, Amritsar, were levelled and it was questioned if these excesses could have been prevented and innocent lives of the people could have been saved. In fact the *Kotwali* police station was a portion of the same block as the Town Hall. There were sufficient numbers of the police force stationed at the *Kotwali* and the crowd did not even touch it while it burnt the adjoining Town Hall with impunity. Besides, most of the other buildings burnt were within a stone's throw of the *Kotwali*. The police had also intimation of the fact that the banks were being set fire to. It was the duty of the police to have bestirred themselves and, even at the peril of their lives, at least tried to save the Englishmen who were murdered.'[7]

The proclamation issued by General Dyer did not escape attention of the Congress Committee. It was read out by an interpreter in Punjabee and Urdu, at intervals, during Dyer's tour through the city, which as he stated occupied two or three hours. The drum was beaten to gather the people. A map was handed to the General indicating the places at which the proclamation was read, and he admitted that it was not read in many parts of the city. 'We have examined the map of the city with the route marked. More than one-half, and that the most populous part of the city was left, untouched by the General. There is abundant evidence to show that very few citizens knew anything about the proclamation. Moreover, the 13th April was, as stated before, the Baisakhi, Hindu New Year's Day, and many people from surrounding villages were streaming in, who knew nothing of the proclamation. That such people did not come and could not have heard the proclamation is admitted by the official witnesses.'[8]

The committee severely criticised the action of General Dyer and held him and Michael O' Dwyer responsible for the massacre at Amritsar. The meeting of the 13th furnished a ready chance and General Dyer seized it. Mr. C.F. Andrews has called it a massacre, even like the Glencoe Massacre. If there can be degrees in assessing values of inhumanities, we consider that the massacre of Glencoe was infinitely worse than the massacre of Jallianwala Bagh, but the standard of correctness, exacted today, was not the standard set in the Military Manuals of the days of the Glencoe Massacre. In our opinion, even the people who heard proclamation, had not understood the significance of the meaning of the prohibitory part of it. Not a single man went to that meeting in open defiance of the proclamation. No provocation whatever was given to the Military Authorities and nothing either in Amritsar or outside it, justified the massacre. It was a calculated act of inhumanity, and if the British Rule in India is to be purged of this inexcusable wrong, General must be immediately relieved of his command and brought to justice.'[9]

The fact that Michael O' Dwyer approved of his action was indeed highly questionable. He was a trustee for the inhabitants of the Punjab who had endorsed a crime against humanity. Even under Martial Law, *de facto* or *de jure,* certain canons of decency are obligatory on Commanding Officers and General Dyer totally disregarded them. 'We repeat that we do not, in any shape or form, desire to defend or minimise either the murder of Englishmen or incendiarism. We believe that they are indefensible, but no deeds, however, dastardly, of an enraged mob can warrant a slaughter of innocent people, such as General Dyer was guilty of.'[10]

The Congress Committee severely criticised the crawling order at Amritsar in connection with the incident of Miss Sherwood. It opined that the deliberateness or the depravity of the punishment could not well be surpassed. Miss Sherwood was assaulted on the 10th of April and the crawling order was promulgated on the 19th. And it had to be obeyed by those who might never have seen Miss Sherwood. 'They might have, as the vast majority of the residents of Amritsar must have, deplored the cowardly assault on her. It was such men who had to undergo the punishment. It is difficult to characterize a mind that invents and takes pleasure inflicting a punishment, whose object is merely to degrade man's state.'[11]

The committee advanced its negative verdict on the heinous punishment of persons by flogging, in public. It opined that such a punishment was not only humiliating but it was torturing and it was difficult to know why flogging was administered at all. Official evidence shows that flogging was administered for the so-called breach of fort discipline, and as to those who were suspected that he wanted to lash them ins the crawling lane. Thus six boys were flogged on the both. Each of them was fastened to the *tikitiki* (triangle) and given 30 stripes.[12]

The committee reported numerous cases of tortures by police of innocent and respectable persons of Amritsar and criticised the ways and methods used by the local administration.[13] "Seth Gul Mohammad, a glassware merchant, was arrested on the 20th April", whilst he was offering prayer, and taken to the *Kotwali*. He was asked to give false evidence. Inspector Jawaharlal caught hold of his beard and slapped him so hard that it made him reel for a while. He then asked him to state, 'Doctors Satyapal and Kitchlew had instigated me to bring about the *hartal* on the 6th and that they had encouraged me, by saying that they would use bombs to drive out the English from the country." The witness refused. The officer then asked his underlings to take him aside and make him "alright". He was then taken away a few paces from the officer's table and asked by a number of constables to please Jawaharlal by doing what he wanted. He still refused. So they caught hold of his hand and placed it under the leg of a cot, over which eight constables sat. "When the pain became unbearable" the witness proceeds, "I cried out, leave my hand. I will do whatever you ask me to do." He was then taken to Jawaharlal again. But he again refused to implicate the Doctors. He was, therefore, kept confined in a room that day. During the two following days, he was beaten, slapped and caned. He was told that he would be made an accused and hanged. This beating went on for eight days. On the eighth day, he again agreed to make the desired statement. He was then taken to Aga Ibrahim, the Magistrate, before whom he repeated the same "untrue statement," that was required of him. Hansraj, the approver, who was also in the *Kotwali,* advised him to do as the police asked. After ten days' detention, he was let off on the condition that he appeared at the *Kotwali* from day to day, which he did up to the 9th of June, when he was taken to Lahore. On the 16th of June, he was produced before the Martial Law Tribunal, where he made a clean breast of the whole thing and told the Judge that he was tortured.

'Brijlal, a boy of 14 years old, was kept under custody for 9 days. After two days, he was made over to Hansraj and was induced to make a false statement before the Martial Law Tribunal, which he retracts in the evidence before us.

'Sardar Atma Singh, a wine merchant, was arrested in front of General Dyer on the 13th April. He was made to walk with the procession and he adds, "They tied a cloth round one of my arms and dragged me along with them through several streets of the city." He was prevented by a British soldier from getting some water to drink. Some others were arrested also during the day, and nine of them were handcuffed and confined in a cell without food. On the 15th, they were taken before the General and were all tied to a tree, "constantly abused and laughed at." After the General had finished his lunch, they were produced before him. Then Sardar Atma Singh was sentenced to 8 days' quarter-guard. He was never told what the charge against him was. During his incarceration, he was relieved by a sergeant of his gold ring and a West End hunting watch bearing his name.

'Muhammad Ismail, butcher, was arrested about the 18th April. His father was also arrested and both were beaten and were released only after his brother Dina was produced. Dina himself was detained for 3 days, and is said to have been mercilessly beaten.

'Lala Raliaram, pensioner, 58 years old, was asked by a Sub-Inspector to give the names of those who had beaten Miss Sherwood. He replied that he knew nothing, as he was not present. Whereupon, he was beaten with a cane, his beard was pulled and he was made to walk up and down the lane and set free in the evening.

'Lala Dadu Mal was beaten and made to crawl. He and his son were arrested, and he was discharged and rearrested, and at last let off, after he had paid one hundred rupees to the headman of the bazaar for the police. He was rearrested and was compelled to pay fifty rupees more and purchase his release. The police used to go to his shop and forcibly took away cream, etc. for their use. His son was detained for 8 days and was then given 30 stripes, although during the process, he became unconscious. He witnessed others also being flogged. He says, "These men shrieked with pain and were all bleeding."

'Lala Rakharam saw Dhaniram who was made to sit down and catch hold of his ears after passing his hands under his legs.

'Ghulam Qadir Toopgar was arrested during the third week of April by Sub-Inspector Amir Khan. He was asked to point out the looted property and he was beaten severely, when he pleaded ignorance. He was asked to give the names of certain persons as members of the mob that had burnt and looted the Bhagtanwala Railway Station. His turban was taken off, his hands were tied with it and he was suspended from a tree for about 10 minutes. He saw 8 or 9 men, besides himself being subjected to torture. He says, "I saw Peera Gujar lying flat on the ground and a *Havaldar,* whom I knew by face, pushed a stick into his anus in the presence of Sub-Inspector Amir Khan. He cried piteously all the time, but the police showed no mercy. For full 3 days and nights we were not allowed any food, during which period we were subjected to police torture. I was released after 5 days."

Mr. Gurdial Singh Salaria, Bar-at-Law, was also arrested. He was one of those, who, in common with others, at the peril of his life, tried to go on the 10th April to push the crowd back from the bridge. He describes also the indignities he had to suffer. He remained in custody from the 23rd of May to the 5th of July.

'The paragraphs, we have denoted to indiscriminate arrests and tortures for the purpose of extorting evidence, furnish perhaps the blackest chapter in the whole of the story of the cruelties perpetrated in the name of martial law. The tragedy of Jallianwala Bagh was staggering for its dramatic effect. But the slow torture of the arrests was felt not only by those who suffered but by those also who were always in fear of being arrested, for, from the evidence collected by us, it is clear that there was no method about these arrests. All classes and conditions of people came in for this treatment. Nobody had a feeling of safety.

"We would here add that we had copious evidence about bribes having been freely taken by the police. But we have refrained from taking evidence on this point for Amritsar, because the witnesses, whilst they gave us their confidence, were unwilling to disclose their names. If the Government wish to know the truth about this class of corruption, we suggest the holding of an inquiry, with a promise of protection to those who would come forward to give their evidence.

'Not much need be said to show that where there was an organized attempt made to procure false evidence, there must have been serious and extensive abortion of justice, during the trials that took place, whether before the Martial Law Commissions, the Summary Courts or Area Officers. It may not be amiss to describe the constitution of these courts. The Martial Law Commissioners were composed of 3 members, clothed with summary jurisdiction and possessing the power to inflict death sentences. They were not bound to record any evidence, and their judgments were unappealable. The Summary Courts, on the other hand, contained only one member, usually a Magistrate, and they became the courts of inferior jurisdiction, having power to award imprisonment up to two years and to impose fines up to ₹ 1,000. Their judgments also were final and unappealable to any superior court. We have examined the published records of the trials before these courts and the statistics published by the Government, and we have come to the conclusion that the majority of the convictions are wholly bad. In the Amritsar district, according to the statistical abstract, 188 were tried before the Martial Law Commissions, of whom 3 were acquitted. Before the Summary Courts and Area Officers, 173 were tried, and 32 acquitted, discharged or released.

'. . . it may be mentioned that cases, involving transportation for life with forfeiture of property as the minimum penalty, were based on such charges as organising the *hartal* or making speeches on the Rowlatt Act. Leading men were charged with serious offences on no better evidence than that of an approver.

'We shall close our examination of the Amritsar events with the remark that the authorities committed a criminal blunder in secretly deporting Doctors Kitchlew and Satyapal; that there was at least undue haste in firing; that, had they acted with tact and consideration, then, in spite of the deportation, the mob excesses would have been prevented; that the excesses were, in any event, deplorable and deserving of condemnation; that the massacre in the Jallianwala Bagh was an act of inhumanity and vengeance, unwarranted by anything that then existed or has since transpired; that, on General Dyer's own showing, the introduction of martial law in Amritsar was not justified by any local causes, and that its prolongation was a wanton abuse of authority, and its administration unworthy of a civilised Government.'

The committee felt unhappy over the happenings in Lahore which was under the command of Colonel Johnson of African fame from 5th April to 28th May, 1919. His administration was so sweeping that it made itself felt by all classes of people, high and low, not excluding the students, numbering several thousands, studying in the various colleges. The tallest had to bend before his iron rule. The curfew order in Lahore became intolerable. Even those who required medical help and to remain without such assistance, and when the difficulty was pointed out to this official by a prominent local citizen, Pandit Jagat Narayan, he promptly stated, 'You cannot wage war without having to suffer such hardships.' 'An officer, holding the responsible position that Col. Johnson did, ought not to have used a technical legal phrase in respect of a state of things, which by no stretch of reasoning could be called "waging of war." It was a prostitution of terms to apply the expression to a state of things that existed in Lahore, or, for that matters, in the Punjab. We have read all the evidence produced before Lord Hunter, and we have been unable to notice a single fact or argument in support of the statement that the Punjab was "waging war against the King." Col. Johnson was obliged to admit that people never made use of arms anywhere. Those who had arms, which they could have freely used, neither used them themselves nor allowed others to make use of them... Many of those who broke the curfew order, knowingly or unknowingly, reasonably or unreasonably, were publicly whipped like common and incorrigible criminals.'[14]

The committee was critical of the administrative decisions of Col. Johnson in Lahore which had made the lives of the local population difficult and unbearable. 'In our opinion . . . Col. Johnson had used barbarous arguments in order to support a barbarous punishment, and this fact alone makes him unfit for holding a responsible position, such as was entrusted to him by the Punjab Government. Nor were these the only punishments of whipping awarded. He has given those that were recorded by the summary courts, but the unrecorded punishments were perhaps more numerous than the recorded ones. Over 170 statements collected by us from Lahore go to show conclusively that the temper shown by the highest officers of the crown had filtered down to the lowest, and in so filtering had reached such a fineness that it was ruffled on the slightest pretext and was allowed to have its full play upon the populace, without any restraint worthy of the name.'[15]

The tortuous orders passed against the students community, in the city of Lahore were verified by the committee. Chimanlal Setalvad asked Col. Johnson searching questions which proved the working of his mind in a way which was undoubtedly highly prejudiced and scornful.

Question: The Sanatan Dharam College was one of the buildings selected for putting up that notice?[16]

Answer: I believe it was.

Question: It was not in the first list prominent, though it was but subsequently added?

Answer: Yes, the list was recast afterwards.

Question: And the notice stuck on the outer walls of this college was torn down by someone?

Answer: That was the information laid before me, not by police, but by somebody.

Question: It is true that all the students of the hostels of the college were arrested?

Answer: I ordered that every male found on the premises should be arrested.

Question: How many were arrested?

Answer: 500.

Question: 500 students were arrested for this notice being damaged?

Answer: And the professors too.

Question: All of them so arrested were marched to the fort which is three miles away from the college?

Answer: Quite.

Question: And during that march they were ordered to carry their belongings on their shoulders or heads?

Answer: If they wanted to carry their beddings, they could.

Question: Were they not made to carry them?

Answer: I made no order as to that. If they wanted to carry them, they could.

Question: On a Lahore summer day?

Answer: It was a May day.

Question: It was very hot in Lahore?

Answer: Yes.

Question: All these 500 students and professors were marched a distance of three miles?

Answer: Quite.

Question: And they were kept under orders in the fort?

Answer: Yes, that is so.

Question: How long were they kept there?

Answer: I think one day. I beg your pardon, two days.

Question: They were then released after taking from the Principal certain undertakings as to their seeing that the notices were preserved?

Answer: Yes, after I got the necessary guarantee that such a thing would not happen again.

Question: I put it to you. Colonel, do you think that the measure that you took was a reasonable one?

Answer: Yes, I was looking for it. I was looking just for such an opportunity.

Question: You considered it then, and you consider it now, a reasonable order to make?

Answer: Undoubtedly.

Question: Your frame of mind, then, Colonel, was as you indicated in your report, that you were waiting for an opportunity to bring home to them the power of Martial Law?

Answer: That was so.

Question: You were longing for such an opportunity?

Answer: Only in the interests of the people themselves.

Question: I do not suggest that it was not in their interest. It may or may not be. But you were longing for an opportunity to show the might of Martial Law?

Answer: Quite.

Question: You got that opportunity.

Answer: And, took it.

Question: And you took it and marched these 500 students to the fort in the hot sun?

Answer: That is so.

Question: And you will maintain, that was a proper exercise of your authority?

Answer: Absolutely. I will do it again tomorrow, if circumstances require?

The committee indicated, 'It should be remembered that the last cold-blooded reply of Col. Johnson was given, not whilst he was in the thick of the battle, but on the 24th November, 1919, nearly six months after he had left his command of Lahore. If his precious notice was willfully defaced by any body at all, it was his duty to make an enquiry, and not straightaway proceed to punish the professors and the students. But Col. Johnson was nothing, if not thorough, and, therefore, he took action against the D.A.V. College, the Dyal Singh College and the Medical College, not by way of punishment but in order to keep the students 'out of mischief', and the order issued was that there was to be a roll-call of all the students, four times a day, the hours being 7 and 11 in the morning and 3 and 7.30 in the evening. "And the Medical College students, in order to attend this roll 4 times a day, had to walk in all about 17 miles a day?" was Sir Chimanlal's question. The impertinent reply given by Colonel Johnson was, "I think it was only 16. I measured it."

Question: And they had to walk like this, in the hot sun of Lahore, for 3 weeks every day.

Answer: That is so, unless exempted by a medical certificate. Question: You thought, Colonel, then, and you still maintain' the view that this was a reasonable order to make an order to keep students out of mischief?

Answer: That was my opinion then.

Question: And still it is you opinion?

Answer: Absolutely.

Question: Did it ever occur to you, and does it occur to you now, it was working upon students the utmost hardship to make them travel 16 miles every day in the Lahore sun for three weeks?

Answer: No hardship at all.

Question: I put it to you again, Colonel, did it ever occur to you that by treating—I do not know how many hundreds, possibly thousands of students, in the manner you did, with regard to the roll-call, you were making these young men bear bitter hatred towards the British Government for the rest of their lives?

Answer: It did, but I came to the conclusion that there was so much sedition in these colleges, that nothing that I did could make them worse.

Question: Do I understand to say that although it did occur to you that this treatment of yours might result in turning them bitter against the British Government, your view was that they were such confirmed seditionists that could not make them more bitter?

Answer: I do not accept your description, but the atmosphere of the colleges was such that you could not hurt it.

Question: Do you think that, by the measures you took, you were helping in the least to improve it?

Answer: I was certainly not making it worse.

Question: Were you improving it?

Answer: I was not out to make them loyal, but I was out to keep them out of mischief and to keep them from outlying districts.

Question: Did you succeed?

Answer: Yes.

Question: You think that is the best way?

Answer: That is the best way, I could think of. There are two ways. One is to close the colleges, and the other is to prosecute them.

Question: I take it to be your view that the best way of making people in this country loyal and well disposed towards Government is to adopt more harsh measures towards them?

Answer: I put it in the other way, by teaching that there is a penalty for such suspected sedition.

Question: Did it ever occur to you that these thousands of students there must have been a large number of perfectly innocent ones.

Answer: Yes, I gave exemption to some.[18]

Colonel Johnson thought that students had insulted English ladies. But the committee found nothing to justify this charge. He had himself produced nothing in support of this opinion, but he had on that account a meeting of the principals of the colleges. He had a frank talk with them and asked them to submit proposals for adequate punishments. The principals came out with what was suitable punishment in their view. He considered that some of the punishments were inadequate and he promptly informed the principals that 'unless the punishments were raised, the colleges would be closed and the students would be stopped from attending the examinations.' In this way, a thousand and eleven students were punished.[19]

The committee also discussed, in some details, the kinds of oppression practised in its veiled form in the name of law, order and justice. It referred to the doings of the martial law commissions. These commissions were supposed to constitute a judicial, but summary trial of persons who were supposed to have committed serious crimes, *i.e.,* waging war. The committee examined the papers in connection with the trial of various Lahore leaders. They were eleven in number, most of them occupying high social status in the society. Seven of them were barristers or pleaders. One such prominent person was Harkishen Lal who stated that he was charged because Michael O'Dwyer felt jealous of his reputation as a successful financier and also in other respects, concerned with activities which were disliked and distasteful to the Lt. Governor. He showed in his statement how insidious attempts were made to ruin the commercial concerns and the enterprises he was managing. He, therefore, stated that his trial and conviction were based purely on fabrication and his deportation was without any kind of legal justification.[20]

The committee commented on this injustice. 'He and other leaders were tried for waging war. We have read the precis of the charge against the accused, and it consists in the accused having taken part in the Rowlatt Act agitation, in the *hartal,* having made speeches, having supported *Langarkhanas* and in being present at the meetings . . . We have read the evidence produced against these popular leaders, and we have read also judgment, and have come to the conclusion that the whole of the trial was a travesty of justice, and it was an abuse of language to consider their acts as tantamount to the 'waging of war.' It is remarkable too that the judges took judicial notice of the state of war in the Punjab, because of the proclamation establishing Martial Law, whereas it was their clear duty, in trying individual cases, to take evidence rebutting the proposition that there was a state of rebellion or war in the Punjab. "Lala Harkishen Lal stated, ". . . the telegrams cost him well high ₹ 1,200, the trial another sum of ₹ 12,000 and the appeal a good round sum, but the accounts were not yet complete. Loss of business meant nothing less than 3 lakhs of rupees." The committee opined, 'It may mean nothing to him lose all this money, but we are aware of some who have been impoverished because of these so-called judicial trials.'[21]

K. Santanam, a young barrister of ten years' standing and practising at Lahore, who was engaged for the defence, had furnished the committee with a graphic description of the tribunals. He described what he had seen himself of the firing on the 10th April and of the other effects of the martial law. He expressed much unhappiness and surprise at the happenings under martial law at Lahore. He stated, 'The consciousness of the humiliation to which every Indian, irrespective of status, was subjected in those days was, however, nothing in comparison to the pain one felt at the sorry plight of those poor prisoners who had been arrested in hundreds, and were being arraigned before the Martial Law Tribunals. It is no exaggeration to say that no legal help of any kind was forthcoming. The Government had, no doubt, out of a feeling of great humanity (one likes to think so at least), appointed a counsel for each Tribunal to take up the case of those who could not afford to engage a lawyer to defend them. But this was a colossal sham, as such a counsel had often to defend as many as 10 to 15 men at a time and that too, without any adequate time to consult them or prepare their case. Some of these gentlemen had confessed to me that in several cases they had not had as much as 5 minutes with each accused for consultation, before being asked to defend them against such serious charges as waging war, conspiracy, arson, murder, etc. The procedure usually was to bring up before a Tribunal a batch of the accused, often numbering 30 and 40 who had never been told for what offence they had been arrested, to read out the charge to them and ask them then and there to name what witnesses they were going to summon in their defence. They were also told at the same time that the Government would try their best to summon these witnesses, but could not guarantee that each and every one would be produced. As often as not, the premise of the evidence for the prosecution was not read out to them, nor were they allowed to take copies of the precise. Each accused was asked if he had a counsel of his own; if not, he was told that the counsel appointed by the crown would defend them. After this, they were taken back to the jail and were not allowed to see even the Crown Counsel till 9 o'clock on the morning of the day fixed for their trial which usually was 3 or 4 days after the day on which the charge was read out to them.

'The second difficulty was that most of the lawyers having taken some part or other in politics, which was anathema to the then Government, were afraid that their turn might come next to be arrested, and did not want to hasten the evil day by taking up the cases of the alleged revolutionaries. The third and the most important one was that there was a general belief that the Government looked upon counsel, who took up such cases, as seditionists and revolutionaries themselves and such a course was enough in itself to get a man into trouble. This idea was strengthened by the action of the Hon'ble Mian Mohammed Shaft, now a member of the Viceroy's Executive Council, whom a relative of Seth Ram Pershad had engaged to defend him when he would be brought up for trial. A few days after this, Mr. Shafi returned the brief, and I have it on very reliable authority that the reason he gave was that a high officer of the Government had as much as given a hint to him that such a course on his part was not looked upon with approval by the Government. It can better be imagined than described what effect this incident had on the already demoralised Bar.'[22]

The committee dealt with the happenings at Kasur under the martial law regime. The administration of this town, a fairly large trade centre with a population of 24,000, was placed in the hands of Colonel Macrae who was followed by Captain Doveton. In some respects, these two officers excelled their brother officers in their inventiveness, irresponsibility and total disregard of the feelings and sentiments of those who were affected by their orders. The first arrest was effected on the 16th April, 1919. Besides there was a proclamation parade at the Town Hall, and evidently, to signalize the inauguration of martial law, they arrested Lala Dhanpat Rai, an aged and respected pleader of long standing. He was detained at the Lahore Central Jail for 46 days, and released on the last of June, without ever having been told why he was arrested. Besides, twenty- one further arrests were made on the same day, three more the next day, four on the 18th, and forty on the 19th. In all, 172 persons were arrested, of these 97 were discharged without being sent up for trial. Of the 75 sent up, 51 were actually convicted. The inhuman aspect of these arrests and convictions was that forty persons were sentenced to be whipped. The total number of stripes given was 710. The flogging post was erected on the platform of the Kasur Railway Station. School boys were also punished with flogging.

The committee commented, 'Kasur was the place where fancy punishments were most common. "What happened was", said Mr. Marsden, "Captain Doveton did not like to go through the formalities of trial and sentence." He wanted to do things 'summarily'. There can be no question of a record of the many punishments awarded by this capricious officer. He 'used to make people mark time and climb ladders.' By way of change, some Sadhus were white washed. Capt. Doveton denied this change . . . 'We totally disbelieve this explanation, and we believe the testimony of eyewitnesses who have described the process. One form of punishment consisted in making the so-called delinquents lift heavy bales in the station warehouse. People who failed to *salam* every white man were made to rub their noses on the ground if they were not flogged.... He inflicted also the punishment of skipping, which consisted in the punished people skipping 20 times without a break. He says that at least 20 people were thus punished.'[23]

The committee was unhappy about the destruction of the valuable property, including a place of devotion by a mob of people at Gujranwala. It was 'wanton and unjustified and no firing on the part of the Superintendent of Police, or even the wicked hanging of a dead calf on the bridge, could possibly be held to justify incendiarism. The firing and, especially, the hanging of a dead calf constituted grave provocation, but they could not be pleaded in justification of excesses.

The inhuman act of bombing at Gujranwala for the maintenance of law and order and crushing the sentiments of the people by creating awe and fear in the region did not escape notice of the committee. It recorded, 'In our opinion, all this firing from the aeroplanes was entirely unjustified. It was begun after the destruction by the mob was over, and the crowds had dispersed. There was, therefore, no question of preventing further damage. We believe, too, that the firing was thoughtless, if not vindictive and the officers incharge of the machines, on their own showing, held the lives of the villagers cheap and fired in order to terrorize the people. The casualties, according to the list supplied and embodied in the statements produced before us, amounted to 12 killed and 24 wounded, and if the loss of life was not greater, it was no fault of the officers concerned. The bombs would not explode. If there was no excuse for the bombing of the 14th, there was less to bring the aeroplane into play on the 15th, because Col. O'Brien had by that time more military aid than he needed, certainly all he had asked for.'

The committee suspected that Michael O' Dwyer seemed to have been the originator of the suggestion of homing from aeroplanes. Whether he was or not, it is evident that he had approved of it before launching this kind of action which might result into a colossal loss of human beings after the gruesome tragedy at Jallianwala Bagh. It is also obvious that the people of the Punjab consisting of a sizeable portion of peasantry in the villages were not accustomed to the indiscriminate bombing. Such a bombing could only be justified in the face of imminent danger to the country by an element involved in highly subversive activities or violent action beyond the control of police or army on the land. The committee remarked with sarcasm that the European population of Gujranwala was in no danger and besides, not a single European life was lost. Indeed, they were quite safe under the supervision of the custodians of martial law who were British officials.

The official evidence showed that bombing was recklessly practised upon an unresisting people at a time when there was no danger, threatening life of property, and when the experience of the happenings at Amritsar and Kasur had shown that the mob fury was a sudden and momentary outburst with no persistence about it. The arrests of the local prominent persons like barristers, pleaders and leaders holding social status and some of whom had helped at considerable risk to themselves to curb the fury of the mob, had commenced on the 15th of April. 'There was at the time of these arrests, on Colonel O'Brien's own showing, not a little of evidence to justify these arrests. They were made, as he says, in virtue of regulation 12 of the Defence of India Act regulations.'[24]

Thus Colonel O'Brien had humiliated men of status and other public men; asked students to salute the Union Jack and ordered numerous persons to clean the drains in the bazaars. Besides, people were forbidden to carry sticks and railway travelling was stopped for some time and the curfew order was issued, thus reducing them to a state of utter despair and helplessness. The committee remarked, 'There is abundant evidence to show that the evidence had been manufactured. The theory of rebellion practically broke down before Lord Hunter's Committee. The only ground Col. O'Brien had to, give was that rebellion was 'judicially proved'. Almost every public leader was arrested. The treatment meted out to Diwan Mangal Sen and his family, the vindictive evacuation of Lala Amar Nath's house, the arrest and detention of people who were never tried, constitute a story of deliberate cruelty which was a disgrace to British Administration.'

At Wazirabad, an important town and a railway station, situated at a distance of twenty miles from Gujranwala, the atrocities of the martial law were incalculable and proverbial. In fact, no *hartal* was observed on the 30th March or the 6th April, but the crowds that had gathered from the suburban villages had brought the news of the gruesome tragedy at Jallianwala Bagh, Amritsar and the inhuman behaviour and tortuous attitude of the martial law administration in Lahore and Gujranwala. These people twitted the people of Wazirabad for not observing *hartal* as a mark of sympathy, support and respect for the people of Amritsar, Lahore and Gujaranwala. They said in clear words, 'Since the people of Wazirabad did not observe *hartal*, nobody would take their girls in marriage'. So after a decision was taken by a huge gathering of the two communities in a mosque, the *hartal* came off on the 15th April. But there were some mischief-makers who were not satisfied with the mere closure of commercial centres. They cut telegraph wires and damaged the railway lines. The mob also burnt the Rev. Bailey's house,[25] including his valuable literary treasures. There was no loss of life. Some of the prominent local persons attempted to check the mob excesses, with more or less success. The committee criticised the action of the mob at Wazirabad. 'The destruction of an innocent and popular missionary's house makes the action all the more regrettable and reprehensible. We have not been able to find out any particular motive for this action, save that the mob had yielded to an anti-European fury.'[28]

At this Colonel O'Brien arrived with an armed contingent of the police and the military arrived at Wazirabad the next day. Soon after his arrival, many persons were indiscriminately arrested and the whole of the demonstration, like that of Gujranwala, took place in Wazirabad also. Two days after this incident, a *Darbar* was held, at which Colonel O'Brien, is reported to have used a threatening language by showing his very angry temper. He treated the members of his audience as small fry and made use of filthy and unbecoming epithets for them. 'Listen, you foolish and mad people, you had thought that the British Government had ceased. Now your madness will be cured. We have got a prescription for your madness. Be it is known to you all, that the Government has authority to confiscate the property of any person, to raze to the ground of his house, nay, if it likes, it can set fire to it. Accordingly, first of all, I do hereby order that the whole property of Jamiat Singh Bagga be confiscated to the Government.'[27]

Soon martial law was proclaimed in the town and how people suffered there under the military law and order had been described by a local doctor, Daulat Singh, late Secretary of the Arya Samaj, Wazirabad. Martial law notices were pasted at different places and on some buildings. These were affixed to the places and houses with which the arrested persons had connection. A set of martial law notices was also pasted at the Arya Samaj Mandir, although the Arya Samaj had nothing to do with any of the events. I, who was against the *hartal,* and took no part whatsoever in the movement, was to be held responsible for the safe custody of the Martial Law notices, as I happened to be the Secretary of the Arya Samaj. Two persons had to be especially engaged to keep watch, and I had to go personally several times to see the notices, that no mischief-monger might tear them away or damage them. Martial Law authorities were very particular that the notices were not injured or interfered with.' It was taken as breach of Martial Law regulations to remove or deface such notices, and the occupiers of these premises to which the notices were affixed were held responsible. Consequently, Dr. Daulat Singh was arrested, and the registers of the Arya Samaj were attached and removed. He was detained for ten days and was asked to give evidence against certain persons, and then discharged about the 30th May. He was arrested once again on the 7th June. He stated how evidence was fabricated against him, how he was given no time even to engage a legal expert in his self-defence, how on the flimsiest evidence he was convicted and, above all, how Colonel O'Brien said to him, 'As Swami Shraddhananda is taking part in the agitation, you must be taking part also.'

Besides, if any person did not *salam* a European by mistake or oversight, he had his turban taken off his head and tied round his neck. He was mercilessly dragged to the camp by the army soldiers and there he was either fined or flogged. One witness stated that although he had *salamed,* his *salam* was not noticed, and he was made to kiss the shoes of the officer in question.

Other kinds of atrocities have also been reported by the committee. Butter was regularly collected for the troops without any kind of payment to the supplier. The climax of inhuman behaviour reached a point when the collection of butter was stopped, and one rupee, which at that time had much value for a common India, per house was realized for the expenses of the army. 'The witness adds that when the money thus collected was exhausted, more was collected. The same witness says that, in addition, 67,000 rupees were collected as indemnity from Wazirabad. He was himself a Municipal Commissioner, and he had to do his share of collecting in his own ward.'

As in Gujranwala, the curfew order was imposed in Wazirabad also and school children were compelled to attend roll call and salute the Union Jack thrice a day. They were also put to great trouble, specially by walking a long distance in the noon day sun. Besides, a number of *charpais* were taken away from the people for the use of the military personnel. They had neither been paid for, nor returned. The committee remarked, 'The trials of persons arrested here seem to have been more farcical than elsewhere. ... All the citizens were sent for by beat of drum to the police station. Minors and *Badmashes* were considered as informers. Anybody, against whom the police wanted to get up a case, was brought before the boys who were tutored to give evidence and thus the poor men were entangled. The same boys appeared before the Commission as witnesses; and it was on their evidence alone that the people were punished.'

Next on the agenda of the committee was Nizamabad, a small village, situated at a distance of one mile from Wazirabad, where people were put to much difficulty without any kind of their participation in the anti-British agitation in a big way. 'There is no doubt that some of men . . . joined the crowd that burnt Mr. Bailey's house, but the punishment meted out to the poor villagers was out of all proportion to the crime of a few of them.' A special train loaded with British personnel was dispatched from Lahore which stopped exactly before the village. The soldiers surrounded the village, looted the local shops, even took out flour, *ghee*, molasses and made the villagers carry these things to the train. 'For nearly a fortnight the people were made to attend the police station and had to sit in the sun from 7 in the morning till 8 in the evening. The people had to close their workshops.'

Similarly at Akalgarh, a railway station beyond Wazirabad and with a population of about 4,000 persons, *hartal* was observed and public meetings were field on 14th and 15th April 1919 as a mark of sympathy for those who suffered immensely in the tragedy at Jallianwala Bagh. Then followed, as at Gujranwala and Wazirabad, the arrests of the prominent persons of the town. A batch of thirty accused was tried, twenty of whom were acquitted. 'The intimidation of witnesses, the corruption that went on during nearly two months and the terrorism that reigned at Akalgarh are all set forth in the statements furnished to us, with a wealth of detail enough to carry conviction.'

Ramnagar, a small town situated about five miles from Akalgarh on the banks of the river Chenab, was also the target of martial law administration. The committee reported, 'Yet the people of Ramnagar were, all the same, not only made to labour under a calumny, but the best of them were made to suffer heavily through a prosecution wantonly undertaken, supported by manufactured evidence led in a trial in which the canons guiding ordinary trials were set aside.'

The committee felt that Akalgarh and Ramnagar were made to suffer insult, humiliation, loss of personal liberty, loss of money and terrible anxiety, simply because the martial law administrator of the region, Colonel O'Brien was bent on 'teaching a severe lesson to the people who had for the first time in their lives begun to realise national consciousness and to interest themselves in public affairs. The tyranny was aggravated by reason of the presence of an utterly unscrupulous local official, Malik Sahib Khan, whose name figures prominently in the statements collected by us regarding these villages.'[28]

At Hafizabad[29] the 'indignities . . . during the confinement, mostly wrongful, to which cultured or well-brought up men had been subjected, betray the degradation to which the officials had made in their desire to suppress agitation.'

At Chuharkana which was an important marketplace and a railway station, the *hartal* was observed on the 12th April, 1919. There was no incident worth its significance up to 14th April. By the 15th, however, people felt much agitated on account of the atrocities on innocent people by the British authorities in Amritsar and Lahore. Some persons, living at Mandi, and others from the villages proceeded to the railway station, and in broad daylight took implements from the railway gang, damaged the line and burnt the station.[30] At this, there was an indiscriminate shooting with machine guns by the military personnel who arrived there soon after. In fact, they fired with the machine gun at the men who were leaving out of terror. Three persons fell down wounded by the machine gun fire.[31] The Sub Divisional Officer, Lala Sri Ram Sud, who made himself principally responsible for the firing, was cornered by Sir Chimanlal:

Question: Therefore, without any further enquiry, you began to fire?

Answer: Yes, we determined to open fire.

Question: Your idea was that you wanted to strike terror?

Answer: Well, if necessary. And we found it necessary.

Question: And after that firing, you proceeded further to station?

Answer: Yes.

Question: What do you mean by moving? They were not committing any mischief?

Answer: No, not at that time. People were coming out and going into the village.

Question: You do not know what their object was in coming out and going into village?

Answer: Well their object was to attack the armoured train. Question: From a distance, how did you know that they collecting to attack the armoured train?

Answer: Unfortunately, I cannot illuminate things which are in my brain.

Question: Pardon me, Lala, we are dealing with what materials you then had and what you saw then. I want to know, when you refer to their movements, what was the actual movement? Will you kindly tell me?

Answer: I said, they were coming and going and I fancy they were collecting.

Question: With what object you cannot say?

Answer: They were collecting for some sinister purpose.

Question: From the fact that you saw some people were going to the village and certain people going out, you considered that they were collecting with some sinister object?

Answer: I think, no.

The committee severely criticised the action of the Sub Divisional Officer which was hasty, premature and indiscriminate due to panic or over-zeal. 'To strike terror was no part of the officers' business. It is a sign not of strength but of weakness, not a vindication of justice but a perpetration of injustices. A guilty conscience alone resorts to terrorism. We admit that the incendiarism, the looting and the wire cutting were all bad, unwarranted and disgraceful, and the culprits deserved condign punishment. But nothing that the people did could possibly justify the random firing that was resorted to and that resulted in the loss of innocent lives and permanent injury to several innocent people, and the other barbarous measures 'that were taken in order to terrorise the whole people.'[32]

In Lyallpur, there was complete and spontaneous *hartal* on 6th April. Wires were cut near Lyallpur, but there was no connection between the wire-cutting and the *hartal* from any person in Lyallpur. Bundles of *bhusa* (chaff) stacked at the station were burnt. This was considered to be the work of incendiaries. Innocent people were arrested and put to lot of trouble and subjected to insulting behaviour. Although a very exhaustive police enquiry was made, no trace of anything bearing on the burning of the *bhusa* came out. The police enquiry failed to connect the burning of this *bhusa* with the act of any incendiary or with any riot or rioters. There were some approvers in the

Lyallpur cases, who were associates of and in the secrets of those who were convicted in the Lyallpur disorders. None of these, however, had any information to give in regard to the burning of the *bhusa* which did not seem to have part of the plans of their associates.

Ram Dass Chhokra, Barrister-at-Law reported that for the offence of reading a paper on *Satyagraha,* he was interned within the municipal limits of Lyallpur and this internment lasted till the abrogation of martial law. He saw the Deputy Commissioner after these orders had been passed against him and asked him why he was being prosecuted. The Deputy Commissioner replied that he had not been receiving good reports about him. He asked the District Magistrate, 'Will you kindly tell me specifically what it is that you have against me.' On this he simply promised to look up police papers. 'I went to him twice after this, but each time I was informed that he had no time to do so. And I do not know till now the reasons for the strange action of the authorities.'[33]

The committee severely criticised the action, behaviour and dealings of officials in Lyallpur. 'The pressure put upon witnesses to give false evidence was practically of the same character, as described elsewhere. A remarkable expression was made use of by an officer to a witness who was expected to give evidence in particular, "Fa *takht lo, ya takhta milega,*" meaning, 'choose between the throne and the gallows.' If the witness gave evidence as desired, he was to be free; if he did not, imprisonment was to be his lot.'

In Gujrat[34] an attempted *hartal* for the 6th April 1919 was prevented by the efforts of a local businessman, Lala Ram Chand Tandon who was an influential person, being the president of the Sanatan Dharam Sabha. But after a week, *i.e.,* on the 13th April some college students from Lahore and belonging to Gujrat, had gone to Wazirabad for the *Baisakhi* festival, returned to the town by the late night train about 11 P.M. They had formed themselves into a kind of procession and entered the town, raising slogans against the Rowlatt Act and the British Government. Next morning they spread the news of the atrocities in Lahore and other places in the Punjab, and succeeded in inducing the shopkeepers to close their shops. To control the situation and maintain law and order, the District Magistrate, Williamson, in a meeting with the local Municipal Commissioners and other prominent citizens asked them to keep watch in their respective wards and also see that there was no untoward incident in their areas. On the 15th, some students along with a few other persons proceeded to the Mission School and asked the Headmaster to close it. The latter, however, refused to do so and also caned some of the students who showed any kind of sympathy with the outsiders. Thereupon, the students stood at the windows of the school and smashed some panes. After this, as the small procession proceeded, they did the same kind of damage at the railway station where they smashed a few windowpanes and a few articles of wooden furniture. They, however, dispersed after they were fired upon. But there was not a single casualty.

The committee remarked that there was nothing beyond the above-mentioned incidents. In fact, no responsible public man had taken part in the promotion of the *hartal* or in what followed soon after. It is interesting to note that the District Magistrate knew nothing about the martial law. He did not want it, and when he received a telegram announcing the promulgation of martial law in Gujrat District, he was surprised to know such a decision of the Punjab Government. 'He questioned whether it could be Gujrat, in the Punjab at all. He thought it must be Gujarat in the Bombay Presidency. But he was mistaken, and Gujrat which had done nothing to deserve it, was handed over to the military and remained under their sway till Martial law was done away with in June.'[35]

The authorities administered the martial law in an illegal, inhuman and tortuous way. The list included some of the prominent persons of the town. Har Gopal, a local barrister and others were arrested and were detained in jail for a long time. Lala Ram Chand Tandon who had assisted the British authorities during the First World War and who held Government *Sanads* for various acts, was also harassed. Houses of respectable persons were searched without showing any kind of court notice to the occupants. A punitive police had been imposed upon Gujrat without any justification whatsoever. A tax of ₹ 42,000 had been fixed and was to be exacted in six instalments[36] Martial law was also proclaimed at Jalalpur Jatan,[37] and Malakwal.[38] The committee reported that there was no *hartal* on 6th of April. 'On the 15th, however, what may be termed a sympathetic *hartal* took place. There was no damage done by the crowd. A procession was formed in which all participated. A telegraphic wire was cut by someone during the night of the 15th or 16th.' As a result of this small incident, martial law was duly proclaimed in this village. Respectable persons of the village were arrested and their number rose to seventeen. Of these, ten were discharged, one was released without being brought up before the court and the remaining six were sentenced to a variety of terms of imprisonment by the martial law authorities. Besides, school [going students were harassed and persecuted. Some of them had to attend the police station three times a day. An indemnity of ₹ 12,000 was imposed on this village without any kind of legal justification.[39]

At Malakwal, on the 17th April, some persons, probably railway labourers had damaged a rail and thus had endangered the lives of railway passengers. 'A train was, as a matter of fact, derailed, but happily no damage was done.' At this incident, Malakwal, like other towns and villages of the Punjab was the victim of the atrocities of martial law. The committee reported that more than forty persons were arrested, including young students and about twenty of the railway clerical staff. 'Of these, eight were acquitted, and over fifteen released without ever being brought to trial, though they were detained for a long time in custody. Respectable men were compelled to pull *pankhas* for the officers. They were also called upon to clean streets and do other sanitary work. School children were compelled to appear three times a day to salute the Union Jack, the railway clerical staff was dismissed, although acquitted. Some of these were servants, who had an unbroken record of over thirty years' service.'[40]

The committee concluded thus: 'We have now dealt with the five districts in which martial law was proclaimed . . . We desire to state that we have endeavoured to keep ourselves to the facts before us, and not based our conclusions on anything outside the evidence, printed separately, supplemented by the evidence given before Lord Hunter's Committee and the record of the Martial Law Tribunals.

'But we feel that it is not possible to ignore acts of atrocious injustice on a wholesale scale by responsible officers, as it would not be possible, no matter how bright the future might be, to ignore the criminal acts of the people. In our opinion, it is more necessary now than ever before that the official wrong should be purged, as well as the people's. The task of working the reforms and making India realise her goal in the quickest time possible would be well-nigh impossible, if both the people and the officials did not approach it with clean hands and clean mind? If, therefore, we recommend that officials who have erred should be brought to justice, we do so, not in a vindictive spirit, but in order that the administration of the country may become purified of corruption and injustice. Whilst, therefore, we believe that the mob excesses in Amritsar and elsewhere were wrong and deserving of condemnation, we are, equally sure that the popular misdeeds have been more than punished by the action of the authorities.

'We believe that had Mr. Gandhi not been arrested whilst he was on his way to Delhi and the Punjab, and had Drs. Kitchlew and Satyapal not been arrested and deported, innocent English lives would have been saved, and valuable property, including Christian Churches, not destroyed. These two acts of the Punjab Government were uncalled for, and served like matches applied to material rendered inflammable by previous processes.

It is impossible, however, to ignore or slur over the inaction, if not the active participation, of the Central Government in the official action. His Excellency the Viceroy never took the trouble of examining the people's case. He ignored telegrams and letters from individuals and public bodies. He endorsed the action of the Punjab Government without inquiry ... He never went to the Punjab to make a personal inquiry, even after the consequences ... He expressed such a callous indifference to popular feelings and destroyed such criminal want of imagination, that he would not postpone the death sentences pronounced by the Martial Law

Tribunals, except after he was forced to do so by the Secretary of State for India . . . Whilst, therefore, we do not think His Excellency was willfully neglectful of the interests of those who were entrusted to his charge by His Majesty, we regret to say that His Excellency Lord Chelmsford proved himself incapable of holding the high office to which he was called, and we are of opinion that His Excellency should be recalled.'[41]

Thus the committee was quite clear in its findings that the people of the Punjab were much incensed against the administration of Michael O'Dwyer mainly because of his known contempt and distrust of the educated classes and also by his cruel and compulsory methods adopted during the course of the First World War and by his policy of suppression of public opinion by gagging the local press and thus shutting out all nationalist newspapers from outside the Punjab.

The Rowlatt agitation had greatly disturbed the public mind and had shaken public confidence in the goodwill of the Government. The frequent operation of the Defence of India Act by the administration of Michael O'Dwyer contributed much for the people to lose their faith and confidence in the Government.

While the *satyagraha* movement and the *hartal* at various places vitalised the people into activity, they saved it from 'more awful and more widespread calamities' by restraining the violent tendencies and passions of the people. The Rowlatt agitation was not conceived in an anti-British spirit and there was no conspiracy to overthrow the Government in the Punjab.

The arrest of a leader of all-India stature like Mahatma Gandhi and deportations of Dr. Saifuddin Kitchlew and Dr. Satyapal were unjustifiable and were the 'only direct cause of hysterical popular excitement.'

Whereas the mob excesses at various places in the Punjab were regretted, criticised and condemned, the introduction of martial law and the measures undertaken were labelled as cruel, oppressive and in utter disregard of the feelings of the people affected by them.

'The Jallianwala Bagh massacre was a calculated piece of inhumanity towards utterly innocent and unarmed men, including children, and unparalleled for its ferocity in the history of modern British administration . . . The crawling order and other fancy punishments were unworthy of a civilised administration, and were symptomatic of the moral degradation of their inventors.

The martial law tribunals and the summary courts were the engines of harassment for the innocent and, in many cases, persons of social status. They 'resulted in abortion of justice on a wide scale, and under the name of justice caused moral and material sufferings to hundreds of men and women.' Besides the imposition of indemnity and of punitive police at various places was 'an uncalled for, unjust and added injury.'

The committee, in the end, strongly recommended for the repeal of the Rowlatt Act; for relieving Michael O'Dwyer of any responsible office under the Crown; for relieving General Dyer, Colonel Johnson, Colonel O'Brien, Bosworth Smith, Rai Sahib Sri Ram Sud and Malik Sahib Khan of any position of responsibility under the Crown; for local inquiry into corrupt practices of the minor officials; for the recall of the Viceroy; for the refund of the fines collected from people who were convicted by the special tribunals and summary courts and for removal of punitive police.

The report of the committee did not escape notice of the press. Whereas the *Times of India*[42] emphasised the *ex parte* character of the report based necessarily on incomplete and not well-sifted data, the *Bombay Chronicle*[43] stated thus: 'It has been written in such a spirit of detachment, studied moderation, sense of truth and responsibility that the conclusions of the report ought to command the universal acceptance not only of Indians but of all Englishmen also.'

REFERENCES

1. They are known as Commissioners.
2. Motilal Nehru resigned as Commissioner on his appointment as president of Indian National Congress in 1919. M.R. Jayakar replaced Fazlul Haq as the latter was called away on important business.

3. M.K. Gandhi, *op. cit.*, p. 527.
4. M.K. Gandhi, *op. cit.*, p. 528.
5. Jawaharlal Nehru, *An Autobiography,* New Delhi, 1962, p. 43.
6. Report of the Congress, pp. 47 ff.
7. *Ibid.*
8. *Ibid.*, p. 53.
9. *Ibid.*, pp. 58-9.
10. *Ibid.*
11. *Ibid.*, p. 61.
12. *Ibid.*, p. 64.
13. *Ibid.*, pp. 69 ff.
14. *Ibid.*, pp. 80-81.
15. *Ibid.* p. 82.
16. Another form of torture invented by Col. Johnson was to paste his notices on the houses of those whom he considered to be 'evilly disposed persons'. The owner was made responsible for any damage done, including, even the dirtying of these notices.'
17. Report of the Congress, pp. 84 ff.
18. *Ibid.*, pp. 87-88.
19. *Ibid.*, p. 88
20. The general dislike that M. O'Dwyer felt towards the deponent was intensified in that the deponent had been appointed a member of the Congress deputation, and was to proceed to England at the end of April 1919, and that he had also been elected to preside at the Punjab Provincial Conference which was to be held at Jullundur on 18-19 April 1919.
21. Report of the Congress, pp. 91-92.
22. *Ibid.*, pp. 92-94.
23. *Ibid.*, pp. 98-100.
24. A notice was issued under Martial Law Rule No. 2 by the Officer Commanding, Gujranwala. 'As we have come to know that some shopkeepers who live within the Municipal limits of Gujranwala, shut up their shops when the army and police go to them to purchase articles or that they refuse to sell the articles to the army or the police soldiers for a reasonable price. Therefore, the under-mentioned orders are issued that after the publication of this Notice, those shopkeepers who would be found acting mentioned above, would be arrested, and they would be liable to be punished by flogging.

25. Rev. Bailey's house stood on an isolated piece of ground about two miles from Wazirabad.
26. *Report of the Congress*, pp. 111-112.
27. *Ibid.*, p. 112.
28. *Ibid.*, pp. 117-19.
29. It is situated at a distance of 15 miles from Akalgarh on the Wazirabad-Lyallpur railway line and was a fairly large trade centre. Its population in 1919 was about 5,000 persons.
30. *Report of the Congress*, p. 134.
31. *Abid.*, p. 136.
32. *Ibid.*, pp. 135-36.
33. *Ibid.*, p. 150.
34. Gujrat is an historic place for the battle of Gujrat during the Sikh wars. It is a Railway Station beyond Wazirabad, on the main line and nine miles from it. It had a population of nearly 20,000.
35. *Report of the Congress*, pp. 150-51.
36. One-fourth of this amount has been exacted from Lala Ram Chand Tandon and one-fourth from some pleaders.
37. It is a small village in Gujrat district, about eight miles from Gujrat. It was an important weaving centre.
38. It is an important railway junction and is reached from Lala Musa which is on the main line and which is over ten miles from Gujrat. It had a population of 3,000.
39. *Report of the Congress*, p. 152.
40. *Ibid.*, pp. 152-53.
41. *Ibid.*, pp. 156-57.
42. *Times of India*, 26 March, 1920.
43. *Bombay Chronicle*, 26 March, 1920.

Chapter 6
New Awakening

The decision to hold the thirty-fourth session of the Indian National Congress at Amritsar was deeply attached with the touching sentiments generated by the tragic incident in the Jallianwala Bagh a few months earlier. The city, an historic one on numerous counts, had gained much publicity after April 1919 when the tragic happenings were featured in the press and in numerous political and social meetings at several places in the Punjab and elsewhere. The election of a seasoned, reputed and affluent lawyer of Allahabad and a prominent leader of the Congress as President was a befitting tribute to Pandit Motilal Nehru. Both Motilal Nehru and young Jawa- harlal Nehru were critical of the great tragedy that had taken the lives of hundreds of innocent persons in the *Bagh*.

Undoubtedly, the session was well attended. There were 7,031 delegates who assembled on 27th December, 1919 at the *pandal* in the Aitchison Park, opposite the Railway Lines, in Amritsar. The prominent leaders who attended this Congress, were Mahatma Gandhi, Motilal Nehru, Madan Mohan Malaviya, Bal Gangadhar Tilak, C.R. Das, Annie Besant, M.A. Jinnah, Mr. and Mrs. Hasan Imam, Raja of Mahmudabad, C.P. Ramaswami Iyer, Hakim Ajmal Khan, Dinshaw Petit, Srinivasa Sastri, Kasturiranga Iyengar, Vijiaraghavachariar, Bipin Chandra Pal, Dr. Saifuddin Kitchlew, Dr. Satyapal, Lala Harkishen Lai, and last but not the least Pandit Rambhaj Dutt Chaudhri. The proceedings began after the President's arrival with a welcome song sung by some ladies led by Mrs. Sarladevi Chaudhrani.[1]

The chairman of the reception committee, Swami Shraddha-nanda, mentioned about the effects of the tragic events that had happened in some areas of the province. 'But where selfishness so reigns supreme on all sides how could unselfishness shine forth. Ordinances gave place to disorder, and peace made room for a reign of terror. Everyone was simply thunder struck on getting news of the cruel bloodshed on the sacred day of the Baisakha Sankranti. Martial Law, however, prevailed and there was quiet—the quiet of cremation ground and the graveyard—the silence of death.'[2]

The promulgation of martial law was also discussed by the chairman. 'The doses of Martial Law, which Lt. Col. Frank Johnson and General Dyer administered to the Punjab have instead of casting it 50 years behind, stimulated its political activity so far that now having as it bridged over a number of years it stands abreast of the other more advanced provinces . . .' In the same breath, he advised the moderates, liberals, extremists, radicals and home-rulers to unite amongst themselves as their goal was common—to achieve self-Government for India.[3]

While narrating the tragic incident at Jallianwala Bagh the chairman had a word of praise for Hindu-Muslim unity which had been shown during 1919. 'Its second fruit is the realisation of the sublimity of penance and forbearance. The Martial Law has well-established the value of character and indeed character is the key to true progress. Its third fruit is a clear vindication of the powers of constitutional agitation and forbearance. The Jallianwala Bagh presented the best illustration for forbearance, for both young and old there received the volleys of bullets like showers of flowers.'[4]

In the end he laid emphasis on the development of the scheme of education and deprecated the tendency of making the students as slaves of western thought and culture. 'When that fortunate day comes, you shall have to give up your western methods of eating and drinking and dressing. You shall have to bid adieu once for all to your life of luxury. Then will the scattered parts of this nation unite. Then will a true system of national education evolve, which would be managed entirely by our own men.'[5]

In the opening sentences of his presidential speech, Motilal Nehru mentioned about the 'recent tragic events in the Punjab'.

He stated, 'Those events furnish many a dark chapter to the history of the past twelve months, but none darker than the great tragedy enacted in the very city of Amritsar in April last.' He called it the 'cruel murder of hundreds of your brothers.'[8] He criticised the British Government for its nonfulfilment of the promises it made during the war. Even after the termination of war, there was no hope for attaining self-determination for the country. 'Peace has new come, partially at least, but it has brought little comfort even to the victors. The pledges made by statesmen have proved but empty words, the principles for which the War was fought have been forgotten and the famous fourteen points are dead and gone.'[7]

Motilal Nehru made a reference about the prevailing situation in various countries of the world. *Vae victts* is still, as of old, the order of the day. Russia, hungering for peace, is allowed no respite and a number of little wars are waging on the continent of Europe. Prussianism has been crushed but it has been reborn in the other countries of the west which have enthroned militarism on high. The fate of Turkey hangs in the balance, and Ireland and Egypt are being made to feel the might of the British Empire. In India, the first fruits of the peace were the Rowlatt Bills and Martial Law. It was not for this that the war was fought, it was not for this that many hundreds of thousands laid down their lives.' He warned that, 'Our rulers have failed to realise that repression and conciliation cannot go hand in hand; that the grace of a gift lies more in the manner of giving than in the thing given.'[8]

Congratulating the people of Amritsar and the Punjab, the president mentioned about their sufferings and sacrifices for the cause of the nation. 'India has suffered much at the hands of an alien and reactionary bureaucracy, but the Punjab has in that respect acquired a most unenviable notoriety.' But repression and terrorism have never yet killed the life of a nation, they increase the disaffection and drive it underground to pursue an unhealthy course breaking out occasionally into crimes of violence . . . No one can but deplore violence and political crime.' He also traced out the past history of the agitation in the Punjab. 'During the early days of Sir Michael O' Dwyer's rule occurred the *Komagata Maru* incident. On landing in India they found themselves prisoners and, broken down as they were by the consistent ill-treatment they had received at home and abroad, they completely lost their heads and the unfortunate Budge-Budge riot was the result. (This) episode marked the recrudescence of unrest in the Punjab and afforded a pretext to Sir Michael O' Dwyer to ask for more 'effective power' ... At last Lord Harding was compelled to yield and the Defence of India Act which substantially embodied the provisions of this draft ordinance was hurriedly passed through the Indian Council. How this "essentially war measure" has been used not only in the Punjab but in the other provinces as well to deal with matters wholly unconnected with the war, we all know."[9]

The Rowlatt legislation was also viewed with severe criticism in the presidential speech. 'The most remarkable feature of the Act in this respect is that no right of appeal is given even when the judges differ, the only consideration shown being that no sentence of death shall be passed if there is such difference of opinion ... The negation of law and justice which the Rowlatt Act represents could only be necessary to cover the inability or incompetence of the Government to cope with an evil which is by no means confined to India. The only justification pleaded is that the Act is not meant for the innocent and the law-abiding who need have no fear of its application to them. But it is conveniently forgotten that the sole judge of the innocence or guilt of any person, however, high placed he may be, is the executive. And who can have faith in the executive if the safeguards imposed by law on them are removed . . . After what has happened recently in the Punjab, and at different times in other parts of India, let no man ask us to put implicit faith in the reasonableness of Government measures and methods . . . The point is that no executive in the world, however competent it may be, has any business to usurp the jurisdiction of duly constituted law courts or deprive the people of the protection afforded by them.'[10]

The president mentioned about the 'popular cries' in the Punjab which put the main provisions of the Act in a nutshell. 'No *vakil,* no appeal, no *daleel.* He explained, 'To compare the arrest and confinement without trial of citizen, and numerous other restraints put on his liberty of action and speech, with the governance of a school or a club is, to say the least, adding a gross insult to a serious wrong . . . The Act is an ugly blot on the Indian Statute Book and must be removed without delay.'

The launching of *satyagraha* was another significant item in Motilal Nehru's speech. He applauded the trenchant criticism levelled by Mahatma Gandhi in his numerous speeches, statements and writings against the Rowlatt Bills. With his incessant efforts, the masses of India were suddenly awakened and the message of *satyagraha* entered the humblest home. He was quite sure that unless the people adhered to truth and discard fear, they could not get rid of 'slave psychology', the outcome of generations of repression which had been our 'sad inheritance'. 'And violence cannot avail us. This is the special weapon of the west and we cannot hope to win freedom by armed force. But even if we could do so it would be a barren victory, a victory which would degrade and coarsen us and make us less fit to enjoy the freedom we had so won. We would develop the same vices against which we are contending now in our turn would start the game of repression.'

While elaborating his ideas about the recurrence of *hartal* on 6th April, the Congress President stated, 'There was no civil disobedience of laws in the Punjab. *Satyagraha* flourished more in other parts of the country and yet there was no disturbance there. The *hartals* of the 6th April did not cause any breach of the peace. It was only after two popular leaders of the city had been suddenly deported and Mahatma Gandhi, the most revered Indian of the day, had been arrested, that the passions of the populace broke loose in certain parts of the country. That would have been so even without *satyagraha* or *hartal*. The disturbances were the result of the action of the authorities. They knew full well, in the Punjab at least, that the consequence of their provocative action would lead to trouble and they took measures accordingly.'[11] He had a serious dig on clamping of martial law in the Punjab which almost cut off this province from the rest of the world. 'It was difficult to ascertain the happenings there and only one-sided accounts were presented by the Government. Outsiders were not permitted to enter the 'charmed area', even C.F. Andrews being turned out of the province.

Indeed a major portion of his speech was spent on the earlier happenings at Amritsar; the operation of inhuman treatment meted out to the innocent local population by the British officials. The sudden deportation of Drs. Kitchlew and Satyapal was a typical act of the British administrators. Having convinced themselves that there was revolution in the air, that conspiracies were being hatched, that the wonderful calm of the 6th and 9th of April had strange currents underneath, they took the only step which appealed to the mind of a bureaucrat. This kind of action, they thought, would greatly upset the people, leading to a serious trouble. Could they crush them with the "ample resources" at their disposal? It did not strike them that the people could be reasoned with or could be conciliated. Nor did they think of having recourse to the ordinary law courts of the country. They do not believe in the intricacies or the delays of the law. They believe in making themselves the judges and meeting out swift and stern justice to their opponents.'

Besides, he severely criticised the violent action of the British government in Jallianwala Bagh. 'But saddest most revealing of all was the great tragedy which occurred here on the Baisakhi day. No Indian and no true Englishman can hear the story of the *Khuni Bagh,* as it is now aptly called, without a sickening feeling of horror . . . What words, fellow delegates, can I use to express your feelings, and mine whose kith and kin were mercilessly shot down by the hundred in cold blood? The facts of this incident were before you, they have largely been admitted by the authorities . . . General Dyer, the author of the deed, has almost boasted of his achievement. He has sought to justify it . . . The defenders of law and order had won a great victory, they had crushed the great rebellion.'[12]

Talking about the crawling orders in Amritsar, cruelties and atrocities of British officials on innocent people in Lahore, Gujranwala, Kasur and other places, he explained, 'In Gujranwala, as you are all aware, . . .act of bombing from aeroplanes was practised, a bomb being actually dropped on a school boarding house full of boys. The manner in which bombs were dropped may be gathered from Lt. Dodkin's statement. He says, 'I saw twenty or thirty people in a field talking to one another and dropped bombs on them. I did not know who they were, whether they had assembled for an unlawful purpose, but I bombed as my orders were to disperse crowds.'[13] In Kasur, Captain Doveton evolved a "fancy and novel" punishments for the people and sought to teach them how to observe the ancient customs of India by touching the ground with their foreheads. He also had men stripped and flogged in the presence of prostitutes. 'His brother officer Lt. Col. Macrae meanwhile amused himself by having school boys flogged in public in order to set an example to all evil-doers. The bigger boys were picked out at random, perhaps they could bear the whipping better. They were not guilty of any offence. "It was their misfortune" . . . All the male inhabitants, boys and men, ten thousand in number, had to present themselves, for the identification parade. The men arrested, 150 in number, were put in a cage placed on the station platform, and a public gallows was erected, entirely at the instance of the Punjab Government, before any one was tried or condemned to death; so Col. Macrae informs us.'[14]

The Hindu-Muslim unity was another significant aspect of the presidential speech. Besides the attempt to terrorize the people, the Punjab officials aimed a blow at the most valuable asset of Indian political life, the union between Hindus and Muslims. The president mentioned the pathetic scenes of fraternization between the two communities which took place during the disturbances in Delhi, Lahore and other places accompanied with the shouts of *Hindu-Muslim ki jai.* These expressions of friendliness and fellowship in a common trouble were treated by the Punjab officials as heinous crimes amounting to open rebellion and waging a war against the king. 'One of the most shameful acts of the Martial Law authorities was to ridicule the Hindu-Muslim entente publicly in various ways. The admission of Hindus to the Mohammadan mosques and of Mohammadans to the Hindu temples, the drinking of water or *sherbet* from out of the same glass by Hindus and Mohammadans were unmistakable signs of a far deeper union of the two than could be looked upon with equanimity by those who were interested in keeping them apart. And an attempt was made under official inspiration during the closing days of Martial Law to found separate political associations or *Sabhas* for Hindus, Mohammadans and Sikhs. I do not know what progress has been made in this direction but I trust that my fellow countrymen of all communities will refrain from swallowing this fatal bait.'[15]

The president also made a comprehensive reference to the necessity of martial law, the cases during the operation of this law and the official responsibilities, in this regard, of Michael O'Dwyer and Lord Chelmsford. He stated, . I think I am fully within my rights in pointing out that the question is not so much whether there was necessity for the application of Martial Law at any time as whether it was necessary when it was actually applied. It may be that Martial Law could be justified if it had been introduced at the time when the disturbances were actually going on, but it is an admitted fact that it is not so applied. What was done was to call on the military to help the civil administration, which is well within the discretion of every magistrate under our Criminal Law, but is very different from Martial Law.

'Whatever the findings of your Commissioners and Lord Hunter's Committee as to the initial necessity of Martial Law may be, there is not the slightest doubt, on the admissions made by the official witnesses before Lord Hunter's Committee, that there was absolutely no justification for keeping it in force for the unconsciousable length of time during which its horrors continued to be perpetrated. Admittedly, it was not required to maintain law and order and the only justification pleaded, besides the old story of the dangers arising from the proximity of the frontier, is that it enabled the offenders to be brought to speedy justice.'[16]

Indeed the martial law commissions, summary and area courts, the President stated, had caused the greatest misery to the people. Many lay in jails; 108 persons were sentenced to death and the aggregate sentences of imprisonment amounted to the stupendous total of 7,371 years and 5 months (allowing 20 years for a sentence of transportation for life). 'Many of these sentences have been largely reduced by the present Lieutenant-Governor. Clemency has been shown where justice was needed. Injustice cannot be tempered with mercy. Sir Edward Maclagan is a kindly gentleman who has tried to mitigate the rigours of his predecessors' regime but he has not had the courage or the wisdom to break it through the evil traditions he has inherited.'[17]

The responsibility for this type of administration, Motilal Nehru admitted, originated, without any doubt, from working of the mind of Michael O'Dwyer who had endeavoured to show and strove to make the Punjab a kind of Ulster in relation to the rest of India. 'To him there was little difference between a constitutional agitator and an anarchist. For both he had the same remedy, repression. But the remedy failed him and increased the disease. And then he played his master card and brought in Martial Law to kill once for all the breed that agitates. He has failed again in his endeavour, but his policy has resulted in death for many and in utmost misery for thousands. For that he is fully responsible. He is responsible for the actions of General Dyer and military colleagues in Amritsar; he is responsible for the doings of his subordinates in the other districts under Martial Law.[18] He also blamed Lord Chelmsford who did not discharge his official duty 'faithfully and adequately'. He questioned with sarcasm: 'He must have known or ought to have known, what was happening in the Punjab. The Congress Committee repeatedly drew his attention to it . . . Has he shown us any sympathy? Has he even been into the heart of the province to acquaint himself by personal enquiry on the spot concerning the tragedies which have taken place? We have not even heard that his heart has bled for Amritsar . . . Has he faithfully and adequately discharged his duty to his King and to his fellow countrymen by his persistent refusal to listen or to interfere, by his aloofness and by his absence from the scene of these happenings, when hundreds of His Majesty's subjects were done to death by the military and thousands put to shameful indignity.'[19]

The process of constitutional development in India was also elaborated by him. The government of India Act, he stated, was not based on the wishes of the people of India and its provisions fell short of the minimum demands made by the Indian National Congress. It gave the people some power, but it did not give them free citizenship or the power to check the misuse of the executive of the functions of law and order. It thus ignored the insistent demand of the country for a Declaration of Rights. In fact, this demand was clearly formulated by the special Congress in Bombay, and it was reiterated in Delhi in 1918. Subsequent events had but emphasised the necessity for it. No constitution could meet our need unless it was accompanied with a guarantee and a clear declaration of our elementary rights which had been so ruthlessly violated in the Punjab. 'No India can be blind to the fact that the protection of our fundamental civic liberties is a matter of the most urgent consequence. No statesman can shut his eyes to the supreme moral necessity of securing the faith of the Indian people in the inviolability of their rights of citizenship . . . Without these rights, as some of the most distinguished publicists in England have stated recently in a manifesto, "British freedom is a mockery." It is obvious that all these traditional rights have been set at naught in India by the combined operation of the Indian D.O.R.A., the numerous repressive measures on our Statute Book and the cult of Martial Law.[20]

Motilal Nehru touched upon the question of Khilafat which he stated was one of the significant issues of the day. He made it clear by saying that 'The entry of Turkey in the war was a most momentous event from the Indian Muslims' point of view. They felt no inconsiderable misgivings about their attitude when they saw that an issue had arisen, which seemed to involve a conflict between their loyalty to their King and country and duty to the religious head of the Islamic World. But these doubts were happily short-lived and the Indian Mohammedans cheerfully cast in their lot with the British Empire when the memorable announcement of the 2nd November, 1914, was made by Lord Hardinge, securing to the Mohammadens complete immunity from any interference with their religious feelings. This announcement was followed by similar assurances from other British statesmen. Mr. Lloyd George in his famous speech of the 5th January, 1914, said: "Nor are we fighting to deprive Turkey of its capital or of the rich and renowned lands of Asia Minor and Thrace which are predominantly Turkish in race."

'Apart from the promises and pledges given to His Majesty's Muslim subjects they have the right to demand the application of the principle of self-determination to the component parts of the Turkish Empire in the same way as it has been applied to Poland and the Yugoslavia. What reason is there for a different treatment of Mesopotamia and Syria, where the population is almost entirely Muslim in faith, or of Palestine and Armenia, where Muslims are numerous more than the followers of any other religion?

'As to who is the rightful Khalifat-ul-Islam, it is unnecessary for me to enter into historical or religious considerations. Lord Robert Cecil has admitted in the House of Commons that "His Majesty's Government have never departed from the attitude that the question of Khilafat is one for Muslim opinion alone to decide." Muslim opinion has now decided it, in a manner which leaves no possible doubt, in favour of the Sultan of Turkey. With Arabia independent, with foreign powers governing Mesopotamia, Syria and Armenia in the guise of mandatories, with Palestine restored to the Jews, with the Greeks securely lodged in Smyrna and the Hinterland, with Constantinople fat-ul-Islam? Fellow-delegates, it is a serious question demanding your most earnest attention.'

Besides *Swadeshi*, sufferings of B.G. Horniman and ultimate goal of the Indian National Congress were stated in clear terms.

'From matters which require political action I come to that which in its one aspect requires no political or legal action, yet which is one that is fraught with the greatest consequences for good. I refer to *Swadeshi*. Mr. Gandhi has made this question his own. He would, if he could, revive the ancient industry of hand-spinning and make the country self-supporting. Modern economists may doubt the success of the scheme in this age of waste and if it becomes popular, it bids fair to solve the problem of finding a subsidiary occupation to agriculture. Seventy- three per cent of our population is agricultural. No agricultural population can exist without a supplementary industry. If our women were to take to hand-spinning and if hand-weaving became fashionable as before, without a big organisation and without a large outlay of money, we cannot only produce sufficient cloth for our wants but provide the peasantry with auxiliary industry. I commend the scheme to the attention of the delegates.

'But, by your leave, I shall say a few words about a friend of India who has suffered because of the love he bore for our country. This Congress needs no words of mine to inform it of the many and varied services which Mr. B.G. Horniman has rendered to our cause. We are a grateful nation and our friends are not so many that we can afford to forget or lose any of them. Mr. B.G. Horniman, as you are aware, was removed from a bed of sickness and without any respite made to leave the country. That is the way of the bureaucracy. Charges of a gross nature have been made against him in the House of Commons and elsewhere. They have been contradicted and proved to be false, but there has been no withdrawal of them, nor has Mr. Horniman been permitted to return. In England he is devoting himself to our cause, but that is poor consolation for us, who miss his wise counsel and his sturdy independence.'

'But what is our ultimate goal? We want freedom of thought, freedom of action, freedom to fashion our own destiny and build up an India-suited to the genius of her people. We do not wish to make of India a cheap and slavish limitation of west. We have so far sought to liberalise our Government on the western model. Whether that will satisfy us in the future I cannot say. But let us bear in mind that western democracy has not proved a panacea for all ills; it has not yet solved the problems which surround us. Europe is torn asunder by the conflict between labour and capital, and the proletariat is raising its head against the rule of the classes. It may be that when we get the power to mould our institutions, we shall evolve a system of government, which will blend all that is best in the east and the west. Meanwhile, let us beware of the errors of the west and at the same time cast out the evil customs and traditions which have clung to us. We must aim at an India where all are free and have the fullest opportunities of development; where women have ceased to be in bondage, and the rigours of the caste system have disappeared; where there are no privileged classes or communities; where education is free and open to all; where the capitalist and landlord do not oppress the labourers and the ryot; where labour is respected and well paid, and poverty, the nightmare of the present generation, is a thing of the past. Life will then be worth living in this country, it will be inspired by joy and hope, and the terrible misery we see around us will become a bad dream which has faded away from, our country, on our awakening to welcome the morning sun.

'But that day is yet distant. We have still a difficult path, full of obstacles and pitfalls before us. Let us march ahead with, truth for our guide and courage our watchword and before long we shall reach the promised land.

'Coming to the provisions of the new Act, we find that a considerable part of this measure is in the nature of a blank cheque. The filling up of this cheque is left to the Executive Government of India, subject to the supervision of the Secretary of State. This process may make or mar whatever benefits are intended to be conferred by the very large number of proposals which are subject to the extensive rule-making powers provided under the Act. There are yet further commissions or committees to come, and further investigations to be made in order to settle details. It is on the completion of this work that the Act will be fully put in operation.'

C.R. Das sponsored a resolution on the reforms of self-government and it was presented in three parts. Although seconded by Bal Gangadhar Tilak, the amendments were shot by prominent leaders like Gandhi, Jinnah, Mrs. Besant, B.C. Pal and Mohamed Ali.

The original resolution was as follows:

1. That this Congress reiterates its declaration of last year that India is fit for full responsible Government and repudiates all assumptions and assertions to the contrary wherever made.

2. That this Congress adheres to the resolutions passed at the Delhi Congress regarding constitutional reforms and is of opinion that the Reforms Act is inadequate, unsatisfactory and disappointing.
3. That this Congress further urges that Parliament should take early steps to establish full responsible Government in India in accordance with the principle of self-determination.

While seconding the resolution Tilak observed, "We are asked to thank Mr. Montagu. I have no objection to thank any body if you wish. But I am not very particular about thanking. We are in the habit of thanking for every little thing. This amendment will be moved and it will be for you to decide whether it is in strict consonance with the principle I have enunciated.'

Gandhi also proposed that the word 'disappointing' may be emitted from clause 2 of the resolution. In support of his resolution, he spelt out his sentiments thus: . . . Throughout my life, I have understood the spirit of democracy. I have yielded to no one in both these things, but throughout my life, I have also found that there come occasions in a man's life, if he wants to regulate his life according to the voice of his own conscience, according to the immutable laws of God as he understands them, when he must grasp and embrace his brother parting with him as a dearest friend . . . My amendment expresses, in my opinion, in more graceful language, what the original clause says.

'I do believe with Tilak Maharaj, Mr. Das and all the other friends that we are fit for responsible Government . . . Their position again was, why should we thank a servant of ours. After all, who is Mr. Montagu? He is our servant. If he has done a little bit of his duty, why do we want to thank him? It is an attitude you may sympathise with. But I say to this great audience that it is not an attitude which is worthy of ourselves. If in the heart of your hearts you can say that Mr. Montagu, throughout his career as Secretary of State for India, has done one thing, *viz.*, he has overborne the opposition led by Lord

Sydenham against the Bill and he has resisted all encroachments upon its liberal provisions, then I say extend to that extent the hand of fellowship to Mr. Montagu. He deserves our thanks. This is all my amendment means.'

Jinnah seconded Gandhi's amendment and observed thus: 'Now Lokamanya Tilak comes on this platform and has told you that we want to use the Act, make the fullest use of it, we will get into the Legislative Councils. We will accept Ministerships, in fact we shall make the fullest possible use of it, but may I know, in the name of Heaven, in the name of everything that is sacred, why does not the Congress say so in its resolution and give a true lead to thousands who are outside waiting to know your opinion? I have no hesitation in saying on this platform that there is a school in this country whose intention is to obstruct and not to work the Reforms. I make bold to say that. If you are intending to co-operate, if you wish to take up Ministerships, if the Act which places such opportunities and advantages in your way is worked properly, then I say it will be impossible to resist inquiry being held earlier. I ask you this question, do you object to work the Reforms so as to make the establishment of full Responsible Government as early as possible . . . . Let this Indian National Congress rise to that height and express its thanks for what he has done. I have no doubt in my mind that Mr. Montague has laboured, I tell you from my own personal knowledge, as no other Englishman has laboured for the Reform of India.'

Mrs. Besant proposed another amendment and opined thus, 'That this Congress welcomes the Reform Act as opening the gateway of freedom to the Indian Nation and as giving her power to walk on her own feet along the road to Responsible Government, thus forming the first substantial stage on that road, and it earnestly begs the people to take the utmost advantage of its provisions so as to reach the goal in the shortest possible time. It places on record its gratitude to Mr. Montagu and Lord Sinha for their strenuous work against greatest difficulties both in India and Great Britain.'

B.C. Pal added the following clause to the original motion. 'This Congress in the meanwhile recommends that the provisions of the Reform Act be used as far as possible with a view to secure full Responsible Government at an early date and it desires to record its thanks to Mr. Montagu for his labours in connection with the Reforms.'

Mohamed Ali supported Pal's amendment in an Urdu speech.

Other speeches followed more or less on the same lines and ultimately a stage was reached when the leading men put their heads together and a compromise resolution was arrived at on the main proposition on the following terms:

The first three clauses would remain unaltered but the fourth clause would be, "pending such introduction this Congress trusts that, so far as may be possible, the people will so work the Reforms as to secure an earlier establishment of full Responsible Government and this Congress offers thanks to the Rt. Hon'ble E.S. Montagu for his labours in connection with the Reforms." This was accepted as a compromise by all except Mrs. Besant. Her amendment was, therefore, put to the vote and was declared lost. The compromise resolution was thereafter put to the vote, Das making a speech clearly stating that co-operation when necessary to advance our cause will be offered but obstruction also when that is necessary for the advancement of our cause. "We are not opposed," he said, "to co-operation if co-operation helps us to attain our ends. We are not opposed to obstruction, plain downright obstruction, when that helps to attain our political goal. The three propositions which I moved this morning remain just as they are with the word "disappointing" at the end of the second clause. Another clause is added which includes thanks to Mr. Montagu." The compromise resolution was then put to the vote and carried. Thus ended the keen conflict between the views of Das and Tilak, inclusive of "obstruction when necessary", and Gandhi's and Jinnah's, that the reforms were to be used for the purpose of obtaining responsible Government, and not thrown away.

In his amendment proposed by Gandhi, a new clause was added with the original resolution. 'Pending such introduction, this Congress begs loyalty to respond to the sentiments expressed 'in the Royal proclamation, *viz.,* 'let the new era begin with a common determination among my people and my officers to work together for a common purpose and I trust that both the authorities and the people will co-operate so to work the reforms as to secure the early establishment of full responsible Government and this Congress offers its warmest thanks to the Rt. Hon'ble E.S. Montagu for his labours in connection with them.'

While launching a severe indictment against General Dyer and other officials, Mrs. Annie Besant observed, 'We indict these officials on their own words spoken with a shamelessness that they did not realise apparently the criminality of what had happened, but spoke it out in public as though nothing had been done. Now there are two kinds of offences, private and public. Where a private wrong is done, where an offence is committed against an individual, there the individual has the right to forgive and forget the injury inflicted. But where wrong has been committed against the helpless and defenceless, where force has been used against unresisting and harmless crowds, where the massacre only stopped when the ammunition was exhausted, when, in a closed space, from where none could escape, the General commanding directed the fire on the outlets of the closed space, until they were choked with the bodies of the dead and of the dying, then it is not a private wrong to be forgiven, but it is a public wrong to be punished.'

The Congress protested against the attempt being made in South Africa and particularly the Transvaal to deprive the Indian settlers of the right of property and trade hitherto enjoyed by them, and wished that the Government of India would resort to repeal of the recently enacted legislation and otherwise ensure the protection of the status of the Indian settlers in South Africa. It was of opinion that the anti-Indian agitation now going on in East Africa was utterly unscrupulous and trusted that the Government of India would safeguard the right of free and unrestricted emigration from India to East Africa and the full civil and political rights of the Indian settlers in East Africa including the East African territory conquered from Germany.

The Congress resolved that having regard to the correspondence between the Lieutenant-Governor of the Punjab and Pandit Madan Mohan Malaviya and M.K. Gandhi, and between Lord Hunter and Pandit Malaviya, this Congress was of opinion that H.H. the Lieutenant-Governor's action is not permitting even a few of the Punjab leaders undergoing imprisonment to attend and sit in the committee room even as prisoners under custody to assist and instruct counsel constituted a serious injustice and that it left no other course open to the Sub-Committee of the Congress to take than the one taken by it; it, therefore, endorsed and approved of the firm and dignified action taken by the sub-committee and its appointing committee to make an investigation and submit a report.

Resolved that this Congress while fully recognising the grave provocation that led to a sudden outburst of mob frenzy, deeply regrets and condemns the excesses committed in certain parts of the Punjab and Gujarat resulting in the loss of lives and injury to person and property during the month of April last.

'Resolved that, in view of the fact that neither the Hunter Committee nor the Congress Commission has finished its examination of witnesses and issued its Report, this Congress, while expressing its horror and indignation at the revelations already made and condemnation of the atrocities admitted, refrains from urging any definite steps to be taken against the offenders, yet, having regard to the cold-blooded, calculated massacre of innocent men and children, an act without parallel in modern times, it urges upon the Government of India and the Secretary of State that, as a preliminary to legal proceedings being taken against him, General Dyer should be immediately relieved of his command.'

In view of the oppressive regime of Michael O'Dwyer in the Punjab and the admitted facts brought out before Hunter Committee, that he approved of and endorsed General Dyer's massacre at the Jallianwalla Bagh, the Congress called upon His Majesty's Government to relieve Michael O'Dwyer of his present duties in this country as member of the Army Commission, as a preliminary to necessary legal action being taken against him.

The Congress offered its respectful condolence to the relatives of those persons whether English or India who were killed and sympathy to those who were wounded or incapacitated during the April disturbances. It also resolved that the site known as Jallianwala Bagh in Amritsar be acquired for the nation and be registered in the names of Pandit Madan Mohan Malaviya and Pandit Motilal Nehru as trustees, and that it be used as a memorial to perpetuate the memory of those who were killed or wounded on the 13th day of April during the massacre by General Dyer, and in order to give effect to the intention of the Congress the following were appointed as members of the Committee: 1. Pandit Madan Mohan Malaviya, 2. Pandit Motilal Nehru, 3. Mahatma Gandhi, 4. Swami Shraddhanand, 5. Lala Girdhari Lai, 6. Dr. Saifuddin Kitchlew, and 7. Lala Harkishen Lai.

The Congress also decided that it was impossible to have real peace in India until the legislation popularly known as the Rowlatt Act which was passed in the face of unanimous opposition in the country was repealed, and it, therefore, respectfully urged upon the Secretary of State for India to advise His Majesty to veto the said Act or otherwise to secure its repeal.

It was passed that in view of the fact that Lord Chelmsford had completely forfeited the confidence of the people of this country, this Congress beseeched His Imperial Majesty to immediately recall the Viceroy. 'It further decided that India was fit for full responsible Government, the Reforms Act was inadequate, unsatisfactory and disappointing and that Parliament should take early steps to establish full responsible Government in India in accordance with the principle of self-determination.'

The Congress protested against the hostile attitude of some of the British ministers towards the Turkish and Khilafat question as disclosed by their utterances and most earnestly appealed to, and urged upon His Majesty's Government to settle the Turkish question in accordance with the just and legitimate sentiments of Indian Muslims and the solemn pledges of the Prime Minister without which there could be no real contentment among the people of India. It was also resolved that no Indian subject of His Majesty shall be liable to suffer in liberty, life, property or in respect of free speech or writing or of the right of association, except under sentence by any ordinary Court of Justice and as a result of lawful and open trial.

'That the press shall be free and that no licence or security shall be demanded on the registration of a press or a newspaper; that corporal punishment shall not be inflicted on any subject of His Majesty save under conditions applying equally to all other British subjects and that all laws, ordinances and regulations now or hereafter in existence, that are in any way inconsistent with the provisions of this Statute, shall be void and of no validity whatever.'

It was decided that the promotion of *Swadeshi* movement to its utmost extent was essential for national progress and prosperity and as over 73 per cent of the population of India was agricultural and poor, a revival of the ancient industry of hand spinning and hand weaving should be given priority.

The Congress appreciated the valuable services rendered by Lala Lajpat Rai to the cause of the country by his earnest and self-sacrificing efforts of constitutional agitation in the United States of America by representing the view of the Congress before proper authorities in America in the matter of the demand for self-government and self-determination for India and requested him to continue his efforts as before.

It recorded its condemnation of the unjust treatment meted out to university and school students in the Punjab under the direct, or indirect, instruction of martial law authorities, and hoped that immediate steps would be taken by local government to cancel all punishments awarded to students without trial.

The Congress demanded the immediate repeal of the Indian Press Act and recorded its emphatic disapproval of the wholly unjustifiable deportation of B.G. Horniman and urged on the Viceroy the immediate cancellation of the order.

It was passed that Delhi should be constituted into a Regulation Province and that it should have a Legislate Council to assist the Chief Commissioner and at least two representatives in the Legislative Assembly and two seats on the Legislative Assembly be allotted to Ajmer-Merwara and British Rajputana out of the additional seats provided by the Joint Parliamentary Committee on the Reform Bill.

Besides, the Congress considered that there was no justification for the exclusion of Burma from the operation of the new Government of India Act and was of opinion that in accordance with the wishes of the people of Burma, the same reforms as applied to the major provinces should also be applied to Burma.

Jawaharlal Nehru stated in his *Autobiography* about the historic significance of the Congress session at Amritsar: 'The Amritsar Congress was the first Gandhi Congress. Lokamanya Tilak was also present and took a prominent part in the deliberations, but there could be no doubt about it that the majority of the delegates, and even more so the great crowds outside, looked to Gandhi for leadership. The slogan *Mahatma Gandhi Ki Jai* began to dominate the Indian political horizon. The Ali Brothers, recently discharged from internment, immediately joined the Congress, and the national movement began to take a new shape and develop a new orientation.[21]

Undoubtedly, the session had much historic significance as it was presided over by a prominent political leader of the calibre of Pandit Motilal Nehru and the comprehensive speech he delivered at this occasion. The president levelled a trenchant criticism against the British Government for its nonfulfilment of promises which it had made earlier to the people of India. Indeed the pledges, he stated made by the British statesmen had been forgotten. He also advised the people to become conscious of their rights and wage a non-violent war to achieve them.

Motilal Nehru showered a word of praise on the people of the Punjab for their sense of bravery, determination, fearlessness and selfless service for the cause of the nation which they had shown at Amritsar and other places through their physical and economic sufferings. In this regard, he detailed the consistent anti-British agitation which occurred in the Punjab on the eve of the *Komagata Maru* incident. This episode had greatly awakened the conscience of the people towards the misrule of the British bureaucracy in India from whom it was not possible to expect fair justice. To substantiate his point, he mentioned about the 'effective power' used during the administration of Michael O' Dwyer who used the existing laws with all kinds of severity.

The president had a severe dig on the Rowlatt legislation which he described as the 'negation of law and justice.' He was also critical of the tortures, numerous arrests and conviction of innocent people without any kind of appeal or *daleel.* This kind of behaviour was labelled as insulting and degrading which left an ugly blot on the Indian statute book.

A major portion of the presidential speech was devoted to the inhuman treatment meted out to the people of Amritsar. Whereas the deportations of Dr. Saifuddin Kitchlew and Dr. Satyapal were described as administrative blunders on the part of British bureaucracy, public flogging, orders of crawling and other illegal orders which led to inhuman tortures of various sections of society were condemned as indecent and brutal in their nature. Besides, the act of bombing on innocent people of Gujranwala was severely criticised.

The president also touched upon the process of constitutional development in India and criticised the Government for ignoring the insistent demand of the country for a declaration of rights. The question of Khilafat and its significance in terms of its significance on terms of its political implications— both national and international—was reiterated by him. The other prominent issues taken up were the condition of Indians in South Africa, Smuts-Gandhi settlement, question of indentured labour, *swadeshi,* sufferings of B.G. Horniman and last but not the least, the implications of the Montagu-Chelmsford Reforms. Talking of reforms, he emphatically declared that Indians would not rest content till they had gained the full measure of that demand.

The chairman of the reception committee, Swami Shraddhanand was critical of the tragedy at Jallianwala Bagh and the martial law promulgated by Michael O' Dwyer in some districts of the Punjab. He had a dig on the doings of General Dyer and Colonel Johnson who mismanaged the whole administrative machinery and used it against the innocent and non-violent people. He was much critical of the prevailing system of education and deplored the western methods of eating, drinking and dressing. He, above all, spelt out the idea of national education to be imparted to the youths of India.

Numerous resolutions passed at this session of the Indian National Congress dealt with the plight of Indians living in Transvaal indenture labour in Fiji, appreciation of the services rendered by C.F. Andrews in the Punjab, Fiji, East and South Africa; investigations of the Disorders Inquiry Committee; excesses committed by the Government in the Punjab and Gujarat; calculated massacre of innocent men and children, oppressive measures undertaken by Michael O Dwyer, sympathy for persons who lost their lives in April disturbances, raising a memorial at Jallianwala Bagh and formation of a committee to execute such a plan, veto of the Rowlatt Act, release of all political prisoners, recall of the Viceroy of India on account of the forfeiture of his confidence of the people of the country, demand for full responsible Government, inadequacy of the Reforms Act, protest against the doings of some of the British ministers towards the Turkish and Khilafat questions, guarantee of civil rights by the Government, freedom of press, invalidity of all laws, revival of ancient industry of hand-spinning and hand-weaving, appreciation for the services rendered by the members of the British Labour Party, promotion of labour unions for the improvement of social, economic and political conditions of the people appreciation of the assistance rendered by the British Congress Committee, appreciation of the resolution of the All-India Muslim League recommending the discontinuance of the slaughter of cows in India on *Bakr-Id* festival, condemnation of Martial Law used against students, unjust deportation of B.G. Horniman, re-examination of the revenue system in India, recommendations for a Legislative Council to assist the Chief Commissioner of Delhi, extension of reforms to Burma and last but not the least, the decision to hold the next session of the Indian National Congress in Nagpur.

The members of the Congress thus dispersed with the deep feelings of sympathy for those who had suffered inexplicable insults, indignities, tortures and economic losses. It felt much concern about their arrests, convictions, deportation and deaths. It made the people realise that the cause they were pleading was for their innocent and non-violent brethren. This kind of feeling soon spread in every nook and corner of India. A few months ahead in the year were indeed most crucial in its dimensions and a most significant decision was made to launch an all-India movement with a deep involvement of the masses of the country under the leadership of Mahatma Gandhi. The event of 1919 and the question of the Khilafat formed the deep linkage of this kind of decision which was approved by the leadership of the Congress party. It was indeed an all-India movement in which the mass participation was a glaring phenomenon.

REFERENCES

1. See the Report of the Thirty-fourth session of the Indian National Congress held at Amritsar in 1919.
2. *Ibid.*
3. *Ibid.*
4. *Ibid.*
5. *Ibid.*
6. *Ibid.*
7. *Ibid.*
8. *Ibid.*
9. *Ibid.*
10. *Ibid.*
11. *Ibid.*
12. *Ibid.*
13. *Ibid.*
14. *Ibid.*
15. *Ibid.*
16. *Ibid.*
17. *Ibid.*
18. *Ibid.*
19. *Ibid.*
20. *Ibid.*
21. Jawaharlal Nehru, *op. cit.*, pp. 44-45.

Chapter 7
The Assessment

Brigadier-General Reginald Edward Harry Dyer fired and continued to fire until the crowd dispersed. By doing so, he considered that this was the least amount of firing which could produce the 'necessary moral and widespread effect.' He did not consult anybody before taking such a bloody, ghastly, tragic and inhuman step of 'butchering' unarmed and nonviolent assembly of persons like sheep and goats in shambles. He gave no warning, a common prevalent legal norm, generally carried out by the officials incharge of such an assembly, to the people assembled in the *Bagh*. 'The soldiers began to fire at once. No warning was given.'

'The terrified crowd, estimated by General Dyer at the time to number 5,000 but which was afterwards agreed to have numbered at least 25,000 people, surged outwards, splitting into two vast waves, both vainly trying to escape the torturing bullets which continued to fly for fifteen minutes . . . Many people were hit in the back. The soldiers continued firing in the direction in which the crowd was running.[1]

It was an act of sheer massacre of an unarmed assembly, an appalling atrocity and a ghastly action perpetrated without any kind of serious thinking. If the existing situation was thought to be unmanageable and beyond control, its only solution was not gunning down the people. Any other solution, far less tragic and devastative in magnitude and consequence, if operated upon after consultations with the seasoned bureaucracy, would not have brought about such incalculable loss of human life.

'The exact figures of the killed and the injured will never be known, whether 379—which was the official version—died, or one thousand, is irrelevant. The fact is that while the government in England was announcing its intention to train Indians for self- Government through political reforms, its agents in India were actually giving Indians lessons in frightfulness to develop the qualities of servility, cowardice, hypocrisy and sycophancy.'[2]

Gandhi wrote in his autobiography,[3] Sir Michael O' Dwyer held me responsible for all that had happened in the Punjab, and some irate young Punjabis held me responsible for the martial law. They asserted, that if only I had not suspended civil disobedience, there would have been no Jallianwala Bagh massacre. Some of them even went to the length of threatening me with assassination if I went to the Punjab.' But Gandhi felt otherwise. He was indeed impatient to go to the Punjab to have first hand knowledge of the prevailing situation. He had never been there and that made him all the more anxious to 'see things for myself'. Dr. Satyapal, Dr. Saifuddin Kitchlew and Pandit Rambhaj Dutt Chaudhari who had invited him to the Punjab, were at this time in jail.

The government officials tried ways and methods of extortion which indeed left a lot of discontent amongst the people. The Punjab was greatly hurt and was seething with dissatisfaction, anger and discontent. The unmitigated force and unscrupulous methods used, naturally, when became unbearable, came in for trenchant criticism by one and all, the Congress leadership did not hesitate to take steps, in a nonviolent way, such steps which should be an eye-opener for the British administration in the province.

Many of the orders passed during the period of martial law invariably caused general inconvenience. Under this category were the promulgation of curfew order, restriction on railway travelling and prohibition against people assembling in greater numbers than ten. In fact, the Rowlatt Bills wanted the government of India to continue to enjoy the same emergency powers, given to them during the war even during peace time. 'We had thus, on the one hand, the offer of reforms by the Montagu-Chelmsford scheme, and, on the other, the Rowlatt Report proposing to arm the Government with extraordinary powers during peace time. The meaning of this dual and contradictory policy was not lost on the people.'

The martial law regime had crossed all 'limits of decency' and the honour of any person in the province was unsafe. Besides numerous rules and regulations were applied indiscriminately and innocent persons had to bear the brunt of the hasty and illegal actions of the martial law administration. No profession was safe. In the words of Dr. Tara Chand, 'The martial law regime from 15th of April to 29th of May was a horrible tale of atrocious dealings—commandeering of transport, stopping of free distribution of food to the needy, convictions by summary courts, imprisonment, stripes, public flogging, marching students 16 miles a day in the hot midday sun of May etc. . . The English officials . . . civil and military, appeared on the stage in their true colour, with the veneer of civilization suddenly scrubbed out. They were gripped by fear, scared by shadows and behaved like animals at bay, ferocious and blood-thirsty.'

Michael O' Dwyer, General Dyer, Colonel Johnson and other British officials, 'exhibited no sense of shame or remorse' in relating their 'misdeeds' in the form of inhuman atrocities perpetrated on innocent people of the Punjab and instead gave bold and fearless statements before the commission of enquiry. All times their replies were baseless and meaningless. But it clearly appeared that all the British officials were in league with one another in teaching Indians the worst lesson of their life by crushing their sentiments with the use of force hitherto unheard of. Misery was thus thrust upon a major portion of the population of the Punjab and they were cowed down to the utmost. The province was desolate by the martial law authorities and the news of the atrocities only 'trickled to the rest of India long afterwards and even then its magnitude was not known to the people of other provinces.'

Before the trials of the prisoners were commenced, gallows were erected in a public place in anticipation of the judges awarding the punishment of hanging. These gallows were erected as near to the scene of the mob outrage as possible. It was elicited in the course of examination that this was done by the orders of Michael O' Dwyer. But before the hanging order could be carried out, public hanging was vetoed. This kind of punishment by hanging suggested a serious reflection. Eighteen persons were hanged as a result of the martial law trial throughout the province, and many more would have been hanged, but for the strong agitation that was started in many corners of India and the timely and firm stand of Motilal Nehru who entered into cable communication with the Secretary of State, and pending proceedings in appeal, asked for the suspension of death sentences. At this, the Secretary of State also intervened who advised the viceroy to suspend these death sentences.

The pledge of Gandhi for the inauguration of *satyagraha* was widely acclaimed and signed. It also proved instrumental for fraternisation of Hindus and Muslims, the Hindu leaders being asked to address the people even in mosques. Here was a unique and novel method of political action by a leader of the largest political party in India who had charisma amongst the masses of the country. His call for non-violent action had caught the imagination of the people who were much impressed by the sincerity of the new leader and the spirituality of the movement which was based on truth and non-violent creed. Undoubtedly, Gandhi's call for *satyagraha* was encountered with all seriousness by the machinery of the Government. It was in the Punjab, however, that this movement met with vehement opposition from the government and a crisis of immense magnitude was in evidence.

There is no doubt that in some places there were serious riots and the mobs committed destruction of life and property in consequence of and as a mark of resentment against the functioning of the British government in India, but their intention was not to put an end to the British government nor were the means adopted by then calculated to effect that. Their acts may amount in law to waging war under the Penal Code, but it was not rebellion in the sense in which it is ordinarily understood.'

The government of India entrusted General Dyer with an important assignment after his gruesome ventures at Jallianwala Bagh. On 8th May, he led his Brigade to the North-West Frontier Province and after three weeks he was ordered to proceed for the relief of Thai. In this expedition Dyer was instrumental in repulsing the Afghan forces operating under the command of Nadir Khan. And soon after the Commander-in-Chief of the Indian army eulogised the services rendered by Dyer in this campaign. In October 1919, Dyer was entrusted with the permanent command of a Brigade and exactly after four months, in January, he was promoted to the temporary rank of a Divisional Commander. But it is curious to learn that in March 1920 he was ordered to resign his command. This kind of severe action against him was unbelievable for General Dyer. He in fact took up the whole case in a casual way and did not bother to engage a defence counsel when he happened to appear before the Hunter Committee. 'The manner in which he prepared his defence—he did not even ask to be shown the specific charges being made against him—his behaviour towards the Indian members and his low opinion of the proceedings as a whole, all point to this.'

Judged by the terrible and gruesome happenings of April and May in various parts of the Punjab, we get a clear inkling from the rumours prevalent at the time that it was definitely General Dyer's intention to 'raze Amritsar to the ground as a fitting punishment for the horrors of the 10th April committed by the populace. Altogether, towards the latter half of the year 1919, the situation in India—what with the appointment of the Hunter Committee with no Congress representative thereon, and with a Reform Bill which was put a poor performance of a vast promise—was not merely gloomy but portentous.'[4]

The political prisoners fell into two classes—the educated and uneducated. The educated persons were, to a great extent, kept in separate cells; for the most part, they were persons who could afford to pay for special diet, a privilege which is allowed to an under-trial prisoner under the rules.[5] They were not allowed to have cooked food brought from outside, but they could obtain fresh fruit, biscuits and books from outside and also had their own bedding, excluding pillows or thick *razais* which could not be searched. A few had their own camp beds, and hospital beds were also given to some of them. For food, the jailor arranged three classes of diet, the prices being about one rupee, twelve and ten annas.[8]

Tan Colvin in *The Life of General Dyer* commented: 'When at last he (Sir Michael O' Dwyer) externed Gandhi and deported Kitchlew and Satyapal, he precipitated the trouble he had laboured to avert. For this he has been charged with provocation; but, as he afterwards explained, he acted on the precedent of Lajpat Rai and Ajit Singh in 1907, and thought, as in that case "their removal far more likely to disorganise an agitation rapidly growing dangerous than to lead to open order.'

It is indeed strange to learn that General Dyer was honoured at the Golden Temple in the presence or a huge gathering. Thus the '... General earned not the confidence only but the love and gratitude of the Sikhs. When he returned to Amritsar, he and his Brigade-Major, Captain Briggs, were summoned to the Golden Temple, and found themselves in the presence of the chief priests and leaders of the sect.

'Sahib', they said,' 'you must become a sikh even as Nikalseyan Sahib became a Sikh'.

'The General thanked them for the honour, but he objected that he could not as a British officer let his hair grow long.

'Arur Singh laughed, we will let you off the long hair' he said.

'General Dyer offered another objection, 'But I cannot give up smoking.'

'That you must do', said Arur Singh.

"No" said the General, I am very sorry, but *I* cannot give up smoking.'

'The priest conceded, "we will let you give it up gradually."

"That I promise you", said the General, "at the rate of one cigarette an year."

"The Sikhs, chuckling, proceeded with the initiation. General Dyer and Captain Briggs were invested with the five *kakas,* the sacred emblems of the war-like brotherhood and so became Sikhs. Moreover, a shrine was built to General Dyer at their holy place, Guru Sat Sultani, and when a few days afterwards came the news that the Afghans were making war upon India, the Sikh leaders offered the General ten thousand men to fight for the British Raj if only he would consent to command them. General Dyer reported this offer, but it was refused, and a magnificent impulse of loyalty was allowed to fade away.'[7]

This kind of humble and submissive behaviour tinged with the highest degree of loyalty, faithfulness and flattery appear to be questionable from a section of Sikh community. It was performed at a time when a few hundreds of innocent persons of the Punjab were put to death in an inhuman way by the bullets of soldiers—under the command of General Dyer. While the whole nation criticised and condemned the action of General Dyer, both publicly and in writing to the press this kind of treatment to the General is not understandable and one wonders why at all a religious place like the Golden Temple was chosen to honour him. Maybe that this highest seat of Sikh religion was under the control of those persons who aspired for more favours from the Government. It is therefore evident that such an element could go to any limit to please and flatter a British army official unmindful of the fact that he was the perpetator of ghastly tragedy unprecedented in the history of India. Besides the bulk offer of Sikh soldiers in the Afghan war was an action which could be expected from the same kind of persons who had honoured General Dyer in the Golden Temple. This kind of flattered loyalty was negatived in an indirect way in the end of the same year, when at the session of the Indian National Congress, Pandit Motilal Nehru and other leaders of an all-India fame levelled trenchant criticism against the doings of General Dyer and Michael O' Dwyer and pleaded for concerted action for forging unity at all levels so that serious efforts could be made towards achieving the political goal for which the Congress had been aspiring and propagating since long.

It is indeed curious to note about the frank statement which Dyer gave before the Hunter Committee. He not only admitted all the gruesome facts connected with the episode of 13th April, but he boasted of his achievements and sought to justify them in the best possible way. To him it was a 'merciful act' to fire without warning on an in offensive crowd because it might have made fun of him if he had refrained from doing so.

The findings of the Hunter Committee reveal the fact that there was hardly any justification for the introduction of martial law in order to have full control over the existing situation which had not deteriorated as it was thought to be. The Committee admitted, 'The wisdom of continuing martial law for the whole length of time it remained effective in the Punjab is more open to objection than the original declaration.'

Dyer indeed gave an unconvincing plea before the Disorders Inquiry Committee that the crowd in the Jallianwala Bagh appeared so dense that 'if a determined rush had been made at any time, arms or no arms, my small force must instantly have been overpowered and consequently I was very careful of not giving the mob a chance of organising.'[8]

Dyer also admitted that he had no idea of the exact geography of the *Bagh* and he was unaware of the exits of its campus. 'While standing on the raised platform, he could see the whole *Bagh* and. . . if the object was that the crowd should disperse then there was no justification for firing towards any other exit.'[9]

Another consideration which weighed heavily on Dyer in deciding to undertake this kind of severe action was mainly guided by the character, thinking and the earlier doings of the people of Punjab whose demobilized soldiers were greatly influenced by the Ghadrites, He had also adopted the nightmarish attitude towards the *Majabi Sikhs*, the *danda* army raised in various towns of the Punjab and the threat of an Afghan invasion. These elements, he thought, were bent upon overthrowing the British *Raj* and unless stringent measures were adopted, there could be no peace in the region.

From the working of Dyer's mind it appeared that he feared at the moment that a few Europeans living in Amritsar might be wiped out by the violent action of the local population if a timely warning tinged with a severe military action was not operated upon. He thus had in mind the earlier violent happenings in Amritsar and elsewhere in the Punjab, when a few Europeans were murdered, banks and post offices were looted and gutted and Miss Sherwood was left for dead in a street.

It is quite obvious that even prior to the firing in the *Bagh* or during and after the firing, Dyer was not mobbed. Nor did he encounter any difficulty which could persuade him to take such a severe action. Two days earlier, calm and quiet prevailed in the city and no untowards incident was visible to the military administration. The burial of a few dead bodies on 11th April was quite peaceful. The plea of self-defence is also falsified as there was no violent happening, stone-throwing or putting any thing to fire.

Puckle, however, mentioned about the state of Dyer's health six months after this massacre. The General told him, 'I haven't had a night's sleep since that happened. I keep on seeing it all over again.'[10] On the basis of this statement, Rupert Furneax stated in *Massacre at Amritsar* that Dyer was suffering from arteriosclerosis and he 'may have misjudged the position, thinking that the two waves as they surged back were going to rush him.'[11] Probably by stating so, the innocence of Dyer is being proved. But taking into consideration his health-chart of the last two years, if not more, Dyer was found quite fit both physically and mentally to discharge his numerous and hazardous army duties. His health, of course, began to deteriorate after this event.[12]

It is evident that the first speech in the *Bagh* began at 3 O' clock. Dyer had already taken measures to deal with the situation. As he had made up his mind to teach the local people a lesson, he took no steps to prevent the holding of the meeting nor did he post any kind of prohibitory order on the main gate of the *Bagh*. Besides he took the command of the force himself which in normal circumstances such a small force is commanded by a Captain or a Major and never by a senior officer of Dyer's rank.

One could ask a pertinent question about this kind of action by Dyer. Was the crowd gathered in the Jallianwala Bagh armed in any sense? It is quite evident from the numerous witnesses including Dyer that the assembly of people had no weapon or stick in their hands and hence they had no intention of any kind of violence on that day. The crowd showed no mood of attacking anybody nor were the violent slogans raised which could provoke the mob against the local administration. This has been clarified by the statement of Michael O'Dwyer before the Hunter Committee. 'Dyer was aware that his retreat might be cut off. . . he went on firing, but he thought afterwards (he was very frank about it) that was not their intention after seeing the place more fully, and that was one of the methods of egress so as to escape from the Bagh.'[13] Ploomer also stated, 'When there was firing, crowds were rushing in the opposite direction'.[14] Therefore, it is quite evident that the people in the *Bagh* never made an attempt to attack the soldiers.

It may be possible to establish Dyer's motive in connection with the kind of action he had executed on 13th April. When he took charge of the whole situation, he was overpowered with full authority to establish law and order. Even Miles Irving and Kitchin were not clear to what extent they had abdicated their authority and responsibility. But under the army control, the civil authorities including the police played a subordinate role even during the days when martial law was clamped in Amritsar. Under these circumstances, Dyer lost his contact with the civil authorities and did not bother to take their help, advice and support of any kind at the most crucial time. The stern action taken independently by a single individual was the result of the feeling of wielding unlimited power. Had he cared to consult the local officials, the disaster perpetrated by the firing on peaceful, non-violent and unarmed assembly would have been averted.

Valentine Chirol described this tragic incident thus: '. . . I entered the same narrow lane by which General Dyer . . . entered with about fifty rifles . . . The crowd was estimated by him at 6,000, by others at 10,000 and more, but practically unarmed, and all quite defenceless. The panic-stricken multitude broke at once, but for ten consecutive minutes he kept up merciless fusillade, in all 1500 rounds, on that seething mass of humanity, caught like rats in a trap, vainly rushing for the few narrow exits or lying flat on the ground to escape the rain of bullets, which he personally directed to the points where the crowd was thickest. The "targets" to use his own word, were good . . . he deliberately made up his mind while marching his men to. Jallianwala, and would not have flinched from still greater slaughter if the narrowness of the approaches had not compelled him to leave his machine-gun behind. His purpose, he declared, was to strike terror into the whole of the Punjab.'[15]

Pearay Mohan in his comprehensive work on *An Imaginary Rebellion* opined that Hans Raj was a secret agent of the local police and that he was instrumental in collecting people at one place so that it might have been easy for General Dyer to deal with them.[16] Pandit Madan Mohan Malaviya and C.F. Andrews held the same opinion. M.R. Jayakar had the same kind of assessment. 'Of all these facts it is suggested that the meeting had been planned by Hans Raj and his associates with a view to making a large number of people gather at the *Bagh*. Whether the authorities at Amritsar were parties to this plan and yielded to it in their desire for revenge, we are unable to say, and we have not enough evidence before us to support] a definite finding. But it is at any rate perfectly clear that Dyer took the fullest advantage of the meeting, in effecting on the inhabitants of Amritsar, as condign and complete a punishment as was needed to satisfy their lust for revenge.'[17]

One question which naturally arises with reference to the administration of martial law is, whether the Crown or the military authorities had any power at common law to create any new offences. According to the law in England, they clearly did not possess any such power. Where it was necessary to enable the military authorities to issue any rules or regulations affecting civilians and where it was necessary to treat any infringements as offences, the practice in England had been to confer such powers by statute. The English Defence of the Realm Consolidation Act, 1914, expressly conferred power to issue regulations and authorised trial and punishment by court-martial. It will be interesting to note that by the Defence of the Realm Amendment Act, 1915, any person not subject to the Naval Discipline Act or to military law, who was alleged to be guilty of an offence against any regulations made under the Defence of the Realm

Consolidation Act, 1914 was entitled to claim to be tried by a civil court with a jury instead of being tried by court-martial.

The officer administering martial law in Lahore had issued a large number of proclamations partaking of the character of regulations and providing for the trial and punishment of persons guilty of an infringement of these regulations. These proclamations merely recited that the government of India had proclaimed martial law and that superior military authority had appointed him to administer martial law. No other source of authority was quoted and while the officer-in-charge was entitled to take measures reasonably necessary for the safety and peace of the area under his command, he had, to all appearance, no valid authority empowering him to create any new offences or try and punish civilians for infringements of his regulations. The government of India, no doubt, was empowered by the Defence of India Act IV of 1915, to make rules for securing the public safety and the Defence of British India and to create offences in respect of contraventions of such rules but it did not appear that the Governor-General-in-Council had any power to delegate his powers under section (2) to the military authorities. We do not know whether the officer administering martial law tried and punished any persons for infringements of his regulations, but if he did, his proceedings could not be treated as *ipso facto* valid. A perusal of the different orders passed by him also created a doubt whether they were called for by the military necessities of the situation or by a desire to strike fear into the minds of the inhabitants by a show of exuberant severity or to secure certain convenient cues for the public or particular sections thereof which could have been secured by the civil Government. Whatever might have been the reason of the regulations, any infringement of them could not be an offence unless it was one under some other law.

During the next year when the clouds of the first Non-Cooperation were visible on the political horizon of India. Gandhi had made up his mind to part with the Kaiser-i-Hind gold medal and the Zulu War medals awarded to him by the British Government for his meritorious services. In a letter to the Viceroy written on 2 August, 1920, he was much critical of the

British policy in India, particularly its light-hearted treatment which it showed towards General Dyer and Michael O'Dwyer. He stated, 'But the punitive measures taken by General Dyer ... were out of all proportions to the crime of the people and amounted to wanton cruelty and inhumanity unparalleled in modern times and . . . Your Excellency's lighthearted treatment of the official crime, your exoneration of Sir Michael O'Dwyer and Mr. Montagu's dispatch and above all your shameful ignorance of the Punjab events and callous disregard of the feelings betrayed by the House of Lords have filled me with the gravest misgivings regarding, the future of Empire, have estranged me completely from the present Government and have disabled me from tendering as 1 have hitherto tendered my loyal co-operation.[38]

Dwyer was known for a violent temper when he was in his teens. Born in Muree near Islamabad and educated in Simla and Sandhurst, he knew India, particularly the Punjab very well. His father had established the Dyer Meakin Brewery at Solan.[19] He was thus brought up in an atmosphere which had engendered in him a complex typical of British character. Like many others of his time, he was taught that the whites were a superior race which had a Divine Right to rule over India.

Even O'Dwyer was of the firm conviction that India could only be ruled by an iron hand and he had displayed the working of his mind when he had crushed the *Ghadr* Movement, a few years earlier, by taking very severe action against the revolutionaries. He always showed contempt for 'educated Indians' as he called them troublemakers. So far so that he labelled Gandhi as 'hypocrite with his ascetic pose'.

For shooting at a mob in the civil area where there is a violent mob in the shape of a procession or otherwise, the first and the foremost duty of an official dealing with it is to warn the assembly to disperse. This warning, according to law, is repeated a number of times on the mike or by any other convenient device. Sometimes it is thus given to the mob to disperse, run or hide. But if the response is negative, firing is resorted to in the minimum possible magnitude, avoiding, as far as possible, serious injury tantamount to death. In this case, neither any kind of warning was announced nor the norms of the use of minimum force were adhered to. The callousness in which the orders were given to shoot down a few hundred persons in the *Bagh,* does not justify, with any amount of argument, by the perpetrator of the ghastly crime or by any of his supporter and sympathiser.

For such a severe action against a peaceful assembly in the *Bagh,* one could remark that General Dyer was one of the unimaginative Generals who probably had confirmed belief that it was his bounden duty to defend the *Raj* by any method however, severe, harsh and violent it might be. One could also say that the General might have thought to win military laurels for himself by silencing the innocent unarmed people to death. Such a thinking or a plan proved a sort of boomerang for him and instead of gaining any laurel, he had to pay a heavy price for it.

The massacre no doubt shot India to its depths but the British *Raj* ended after a consistent struggle for about two-and-a-half decades till it achieved its desired goal in 1947.

REFERENCES

1. Rupert Furneaux, *Massacre at Amritsar,* London, 1963, p. 20.
2. Tara Chand, *History of the Freedom Movement in India*, Vol. Ill, New Delhi, 1972, p. 480.
3. M.K. Gandhi, *op. cit.,* p. 522.
4. B. Pattabhi Sitaramayya, *The History of the Indian National Congress,* Vol. I, 1885-1935, Bombay, 1946, p. 177.
5. Home Pol. Deposit, August 1919, File 16.
6. *Ibid.*
7. Ian Colvin, *The Life of General Dyer,* London, 1931, pp. 201-02.
8. Disorders Inquiry Committee, Vol. Ill, p. 203.
9. V.N. Datta, *op. cit.,* p. 158.
10. Quoted in Edward Thompson, *A Letter from India,* London, 1932, p. 102.
11. Rupert Furneaux, *op. cit.,* p. 177.
12. Dyer was fifty-five years old in 1919.
13. Disorders Inquiry Committee, Vol. VI, p. 68.

14. *Ibid.,* Vol. Ill, p. 36.
15. Valentine Chirol, *op. cit.,* Vol. II, pp. 177-78.
16. Pearay Mohan, *An Imaginary Rebellion,* Lahore, pp. 17 ff.
17. See *M.R. Jayakar Papers*, No. 477.
18. Home Department, Political Deposit, August 1920, No. 18.
19. Now it is called Mohan Meakin Brewery.

Bibliography

Primary Sources

Home Political A, 1919-20.

Home Political (Deposit), 1919-20.

Home Political (Deposit B), 1919-20.

Debates, House of Commons, 1919-20.

Debates, Legislative Assembly, 1919-20.

Debates, Punjab Legislative Council, 1919-20.

Published Records and Documents

Congress Presidential Addresses, 1917-1919.

Disorders Inquiry Committee Evidence, Vols. I-V, Calcutta. 1920.

Disorders Inquiry Committee Report, 1920.

Report and Evidence of the Punjab Sub-Committee of Indian National Congress, 1920.

Report on Indian Constitutional Reforms, 1918.

Selected Works of Jawaharlal Nehru, ed. S. Gopal, Vols. I-III.

The Collected Works of Mahatma Gandhi, Vols. 20-22.

Newspapers and Periodicals

Amrita Bazar Patrika

The Bombay Chronicle

The Indian Review Journal of Indian History

The Leader

The Modern Review

The Pioneer

Proceedings of Indian History Congress

The Tribune

Private Papers

Chelmsford Papers

Gandhi Papers

Jayakar Papers

Montague Papers

Nehru Papers

Other Works

Ahluwalia, M.M., *Freedom Struggle in India, 1858-1919,* Delhi, 1965.

Ali, Muhammad, *My Life Fragment,* Lahore, 1944.

Andrews, C.F., *How India Can Be Free?* Madras, 1921.

———, *The Indian Problems*, Madras, 1921.

Antonova, K., Bongard-Levin, G. and Kotovsky, G., *A History of India,* Vol. II, Moscow, 1978.

Baldwin Hanson W., *World War I,* London, 1963.

Barns, Margarita, *India Today and Tomorrow,* London, 1937.

Bevan, E., Thoughts On Indian Discontents, London, 1929.

Bipan Chandra, Rise and Growth of Economic Nationalism in India, Delhi, 1966.

———, *Nationalism and Communalism in Modern India,* Delhi, 1979.

Birla, G.D., *In the Shadow of the Mahatma: A Personal Memoir,* Bombay, 1968.

Besant, Annie, *The Birth of New India,* Madras, 1917.

Bondurant, Joan V., *Conquest of Violence: The Gandhian Philosophy of Conflict*, Bombay, 1959.

Bose, S.C., *The Indian Struggle, 1920-42*, New York, 1964.

Brecher, Michael, *Nehru: A Political Biography,* London, 1959.

Brockway, A.F., *India and Its Government*, Madras, 1921.

———, *The Indian Crisis*, London, 1930.

Brown, Judith, M., *Gandhi's Rise to Power: Indian Politics, 1915-22*, London, 1972.

Bryant, J.F., *Gandhi and the Indianization of the Empire,* Cambridge, 1924.

Buch, M.A., *The Development of Contemporary Political Thought*, 3 Vols., Baroda, 1938.

Caveeshar, S.S., *India's Fight for Freedom,* Lahore, 1936.

Chatterjee, Ramananda (ed.), *Towards Home Rule,* Part II, Calcutta, 1917.

Chesney, G.M., *India Under Experiment,* London, 1918.

Chirol, Valentine, *Indian Unrest,* London, 1910.

Chintamani, C.Y., *Indian Politics Since the Mutiny,* Allahabad, 1947.

Colvin, Ian, *The Life of General Dyer,* London, 1929.

Coupland, R., *Britain and India, 1600-1941*, London, 1941.

———, *The Indian Problem, 1833-1935*, London, 1942.

———, *The Goal of British Rule in India*, London, 1948.

Das, M.N., *The Political Philosophy of Jawaharlal Nehru*, London, 1961.

Datta, V.N., *Jallianwala Bagh,* Ludhiana, 1969.

Diwakar, R.R., *Satyagraha in Action,* Calcutta, 1949.

Dutt, K. Iswara, *Congress Cyclopaedia,* Vol. I, Delhi, n.d.

Dutt, R.P., *India Today,* London, 1940.

Dutt, Romesh Chandra, *The Economic History of India in the Victorian Age*, Vol. II.

Dwyer, Michael O.' *India As I Knew It,* London, 1925.

Fein, Helen, *Imperial Crime and Punishment: The Massacre at Jallianwala Bagh and British Judgment, 1919-20*, Honolulu, 1977.

Fischer, Louis, *The Life of Mahatma Gandhi,* London, 1962.

Furneaux, Rupert, *Massacre at Amritsar,* London, 1963.

Gandhi, M.K., *Hind Swaraj,* Madras, 1921.

———, *My Experiments with Truth*, Ahmedabad, 1948.

———, *Non-Violent Resistance*, New York, 1951.

Gopal, Ram, *Indian Muslims: A Political History*, London, 1959.

Ghosh, A.K., *Lord Chelmsford's Viceroyalty*, Madras, 1921.

Gopal, S., *British Policy in India, 1858-1905*, Cambridge, 1965.

———, *Jawaharlal Nehru: A Biography*, Vol. I, London, 1975.

Greenberger, Allan, *The British Image of India*, London, 1969.

Griffiths, P.J., *The British Impact of India*, London, 1965.

Horne, E.A., *The Political System of British India*, Oxford, 1922.

Hoyland, John S., *The Case of India*, London, 1929.

Jayakar, M.R., *The Story of My Life*, Vol. I, Bombay, 1928.

Johnston, Hugh, *The Voyage of the Kamagata Maru: The Sikh Challenge to Canada's Colour Bar*, Delhi, 1979.

Kamath, M.S., *The Home Rule League*, Madras, 1927.

Keer, Dhananjay, *Lokamanya Tilak: Father of Our Freedom Struggle*, Bombay, 1958.

———, *Mahatma Gandhi: Political Saint and Unarmed, Prophet*, Bombay, 1973.

Keith, A.B., *A Constitutional History of India*, Allahabad, 1961.

Kenworthy, J.M., *India: A Warning*, London, 1931.

Khaliquzzaman, Choudhry, *Pathway to Pakistan*, Lahore, 1961.

Kidwai, M.H., *Swaraj and How to Obtain It*, Lucknow, 1924.

Kripalani, J.B., *Gandhi: His Life and Thought*, Delhi, 1970.

Lai Bahadur, *The Muslim League*, Agra, 1954.

Lawton, Lanceton, *Empire of the East*, Part II, London, 1912.

Leigh, M.S., *The Punjab and the War*, Lahore, 1922.

Lothian, Arthur Cunningham, *Kingdoms of Yesterday*, London, 1951.

Lovett, Verney, *A History of the Nationalist Movement in India*, 1921.

Low, D.A. (ed.), *Soundings in Modern South Asian History, London*, 1968.

Majumdar, R.C., *History of the Freedom Movement in India,* Vol. II, Calcutta, 1963.

Malaviya, Kapil Deva, *Open Rebellion in the Punjab,* Allahabad 1919.

Masani, R.P., *Britain in India,* Oxford University Press, 1950.

McMunn, George, *Turmoil and Tragedy in India, 1919 and After,* London, 1935.

Mehrotra, S.R., *Towards Indian Freedom and Partition*, Delhi, 1979.

Meston, Lord, *India and the Empire,* London, 1924.

———, *Nationhood for India*, Oxford, 1931.

Mishra, D.P., *The History of Freedom Movement in Madhya Pradesh*, Nagpur, 1956.

Mody, H.P., *The Political Future of India*, London, 1908.

Montagu, E.S., *An Indian Diary,* London, 1930.

Moon, Penderel, *Divide and Quit,* London, 1961.

Moore, R.J., *Crisis in Indian Unity, 1917-40*, London, 1974.

Mosley, Leonard, *The Last Days of the British Raj*, London, 1962.

Munshi, K.M., *Indian Constitutional Documents: Pilgrimage to Freedom*, Vol. I, Bombay, 1961.

Naidis, Mark, *India,* New York, 1966.

Nair, Sankaran, *Gandhi and Anarchy,* Indore, n.d.

Naoroji, Dadabhai, *Poverty and Un-British Rule in India,* Delhi, 1962.

Orwell, George, *Shooting An Elephant,* London, 1927.

Pal, B.C., *The Spirit of Indian Nationalism*, London, 1910.

———, *Swaraj: The Goal and the Way*, Madras, 1921.

———, *Swadeshi and Swaraj*, Calcutta, 1954.

Parmanand, Bhai, *The Story of My Life,* Lahore, 1934.

Patil, V.T., *Nehru and the Freedom Movement*, Delhi, 1977.

Paul, K.T., *The British Connection with India*, London, 1927.

Pearey Mohan, *An Imaginary Rebellion*, Lahore, 1920.

Philips, C.H., *India,* London, 1949.

Pole, D.G., *India in Transition*, 1932.

Pradhan, R.G., *India's Struggle for Swaraj*, Madras, 1930.

Rai, Lajpat, *The Political Future of India*, New York, 1919.

Raja Ram, *The Jallianwala Bagh Massacre: A Premeditated Plan*, Chandigarh, 1969.

Rajendra Prasad, *An Autobiography,* Bombay, 1957.

Ravinder Kumar (ed.), *Essays on Gandhian Politics: The Rowlatt Satyagraha of 1919*, Oxford, 1971.

Reynolds, Reginald, *The White Sahibs in India,* London, 1937.

Richards, Philip Ernest, *Indian Dust,* London, 1932.

Rutherford, V.H., *Modern India: The Problems and Their Solutions*, London, 1927.

Sampurnanand, *Memoirs and Reflections,* Bombay, 1962.

Sapru, Tej Bahadur, *The Indian Constitution,* Madras, 1926.

Segal, Ronald, *The Crisis of India,* London, 1965.

Setalvad, C.H., *Recollections and Reflections*, Bombay, 1946.

Shah, M., *Some Important Indian Problems*, Lahore, 1930.

Sharp, Gene, *Gandhi Wields the Weapon of Moral Power*, Ahmedabad, 1960.

———, *The Politics of Non-Violent Action*, Boston, 1972.

Singh, Gulab, *Under the Shadow of Gallows*, Delhi, 1964.

Singh, Khushwant and Singh, Satinder, *Ghadar, 1915*, New Delhi, 1966.

Singh, Randhir, *Ghadar Heroes,* Bombay, 1945.

Sitaramayya, B. Pattabhi, *History of the Indian National Congress, 1885-1935*, Vol. I, Bombay, 1946.

Smith, W.R., *Nationalism and Reform in India*, London, 1973.

Spear, Percival, *A History of India,* Vol. II, London, 1965.

Srinivas, M.N., *Social Change in Modern India,* Berkeley, 1966.

Stokes, S.E., *National Self-realization,* Madras, 1921.

Swinson, Arthur, *Six Minutes to Sunset,* London, 1964.

Tara Chand, *History of Freedom Movement in India*, Vol. Ill, Delhi, 1973.

Tendulkar, D.G., *Mahatma: Life of Mohandas Karamchand Gandhi*, Vols. I-III, Delhi, 1961.

Thompson, Edward, *The Reconstruction of India*, London, 1930.

———, *A Letter from India*, London, 1932.

Tilak, B.G., *Speeches of Bal Gangadhar Tilak*, Madras, 1918.

Topa, I.N., *The Growth and Development of National Thought in India*, Hamburg, 1930.

Wayley, S.D., *Edwin Montagu*, London, 1964.

Wolpert, Stanley, *Tilak and Gokhale: Revolution and Reform in the Making of Modern India*, Berkeley, 1962.

Index